FOUNDATIONS

Second Edition

ACTIVITY WORKBOOK

Steven J. Molinsky • Bill Bliss

Contributing Author
Dorothy Lynde

W9-BSY-836

PEARSON
Longman

Foundations Activity Workbook, second edition

Pearson Education, 10 Bank Street, White Plains, NY 10606

Editorial director: Pam Fishman
Vice president, director of design and production: Rhea Banker
Director of electronic production: Aliza Greenblatt
Director of manufacturing: Patrice Fraccio
Senior manufacturing manager: Edith Pullman
Director of marketing: Oliva Fernandez
Production editor: Diane Cipollone
Senior digital layout specialist: Lisa Ghiozzi
Text design: Wendy Wolf
Cover design: Wanda España, Wee Design Group; Warren
    Fischbach; Wendy Wolf
Realia creation: Lisa Ghiozzi
Illustrations: Richard E. Hill

ISBN 0-13-227555-4

Longman on the Web
Longman.com offers online resources for teachers
and students.
Access our Companion Websites, our online catalog,
and our local offices around the world.
Visit us at longman.com.

Printed in the United States of America
 7 8 9 10 V001 12 11 10

Contents

A WHAT'S THE WORD?

name	meet	Nice
Hello	you	Hi

A. _____Hello_____ [1]. My _____ [2] is Angela Montero.

B. _____ [3]. I'm Peter Cheng. Nice to _____ [4] you.

A. _____ [5] to meet _____ [6], too.

B WHAT'S THE WORD?

is	you	Hello	I'm	My	to

A. Hi. _____My_____ [1] name _____ [2] David Lane.

B. _____ [3]. _____ [4] Nancy Johnson.

A. Nice _____ [5] meet you.

B. Nice to meet _____ [6], too.

C FIRST OR LAST?

first	last

1. My _____last_____ name is Cheng.

2. My _____ name is Peter.

3. My _____ name is Angela.

4. My _____ name is Montero.

D WHAT'S THE LETTER?

Z   C   V   L   E   T   G   Q   M

1. A B _C_

2. D ___ F

3. ___ H I

4. J K ___

5. ___ N O

6. P ___ R

7. S ___ U

8. ___ W X

9. Y ___

E WHAT'S THE LETTER?

V   Z   R   M   B   T   H   O   F   D   J   A

1. _B_ C

2. L ___

3. ___ E

4. ___ B

5. S ___

6. ___ I

7. N ___

8. Q ___

9. ___ G

10. Y ___

11. ___ K

12. ___ W

F LISTENING

Listen and circle the word you hear.

1. (Hello)   Hi

2. first   last

3. first   last

4. I'm   My

5. you   too

6. My   Nice

G WHAT ARE THEY SAYING?

Complete the conversation. Practice it with another student.

> **A.** Hello. My name is _____ _____.
>
> **B.** Hi. I'm _____ _____. Nice to meet you.
>
> **A.** Nice to meet you, too.

A WHAT'S THE ANSWER?

1. What's your first name?   V-E-R-O-N-I-C-A.

2. What's your last name?   Veronica.

3. How do you spell your first name?   G-O-M-E-Z.

4. How do you spell your last name?   Gomez.

B MISSING LETTERS

Find the missing letters.

ABCDFGHIKLMNOQRSTVWXZ

The missing letters are: ____ ____ ____ ____ ____

C MISSING LETTERS AND WORDS

Write the missing letters.

A B _C_ D _E_ F G H _I_ J K L M _N_ O P Q R S T U V W X Y Z

A B C D E F G H I J K L M N ___ P Q R S ___ U V W X Y Z

A B C D ___ F G H I J K L ___ N O P Q R S ___ U V W X Y Z

A B C D E F G H I J K L M N ___ P Q R S T ___ V W X ___ Z

What words do the letters spell?

_N_ _I_ _C_ _E_   ___ ___   ___ ___ _E_ ___   ___ ___ ___

Listen and write the missing letters.

1. W A _T_ S O N

2. __ A N I __ L

3. G __ O __ __ A

4. P __ __ E R __ __ N

5. __ O __ E R

6. __ O U N __

7. __ O __ T E R __

8. __ I __ U E R __ A

| Hi | Hello | last | name | nice | meet | My | to |

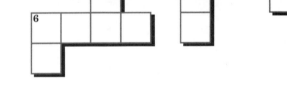

Across

3. _____ to meet you.

4. What's your _____ name?

6. Nice to _____ you.

Down

1. _____. I'm Julie Wong.

2. _____. I'm Robert Carter.

3. My _____ is Emily Park.

5. Nice _____ meet you.

6. _____ name is George Crane.

A WRITE THE NUMBERS

eight	seven	two	nine	three	ten
four	six	zero	one	five	

9 ___nine___   1 _____   3 _____

5 _____   7 _____   8 _____

2 _____   10 _____   6 _____

4 _____   0 _____

B CROSSWORD

correct   number   Yes   your   telephone

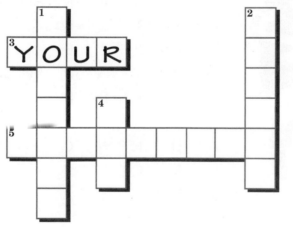

Across

3. What's _____ telephone number?

5. My _____ number is 273–6450.

Down

1. That's _____.

2. What's your telephone _____?

4. _____. That's correct.

Listen and write the numbers you hear.

1. 2 _6_ 1 – 5 8 ___ 4

2. 9 ___ ___ – 5 8 6 4

3. 8 3 ___ – 7 ___ 4 4

4. 5 ___ 7 – 6 7 0 ___

5. 9 ___ 1 – 4 2 0 ___

6. 7 7 7 – 8 2 ___ ___

7. 4 2 1 – ___ 0 ___ 5

8. 6 4 ___ – ___ 4 0 ___

9. 3 5 3 – 1 1 ___ ___

10. 4 6 2 – ___ ___ 9 6

11. ___ ___ 7 – 4 9 4 9

12. 6 6 ___ – 5 ___ 3 3

D NUMBER SEARCH

| zero | one | two | three | four | five | six | seven | eight | nine | ten |

A	L	T	K	E	R	E	F	M	O	K	L
C	Z	E	R	O	S	I	A	P	M	Z	T
L	W	A	F	T	M	G	L	U	V	P	W
I	T	E	N	R	Y	H	L	U	V	A	O
N	C	R	I	N	N	T	V	P	Q	I	G
I	P	T	Z	P	I	G	K	C	U	R	P
T	H	R	E	E	N	S	E	V	E	N	O
S	B	Y	A	R	E	B	R	O	T	O	X
I	F	Y	R	L	I	R	O	R	T	R	O
I	O	N	E	S	C	O	F	Q	C	T	X
A	U	H	N	C	F	S	I	X	H	T	E
W	R	C	T	V	C	H	V	W	C	L	I
S	U	J	S	A	I	B	E	R	O	Y	O

E WRITE THE NUMBERS

1. _three_

2. _____

3. _____

4. _____

5. _____

6. _____

A WHAT'S THE WORD?

| Street say 9 address What's |

A. ___What's___ [1] your _____[2]?

B. 9 Main _____[3].

A. Did you _____[4] 5 Main Street?

B. No. _____[5] Main Street.

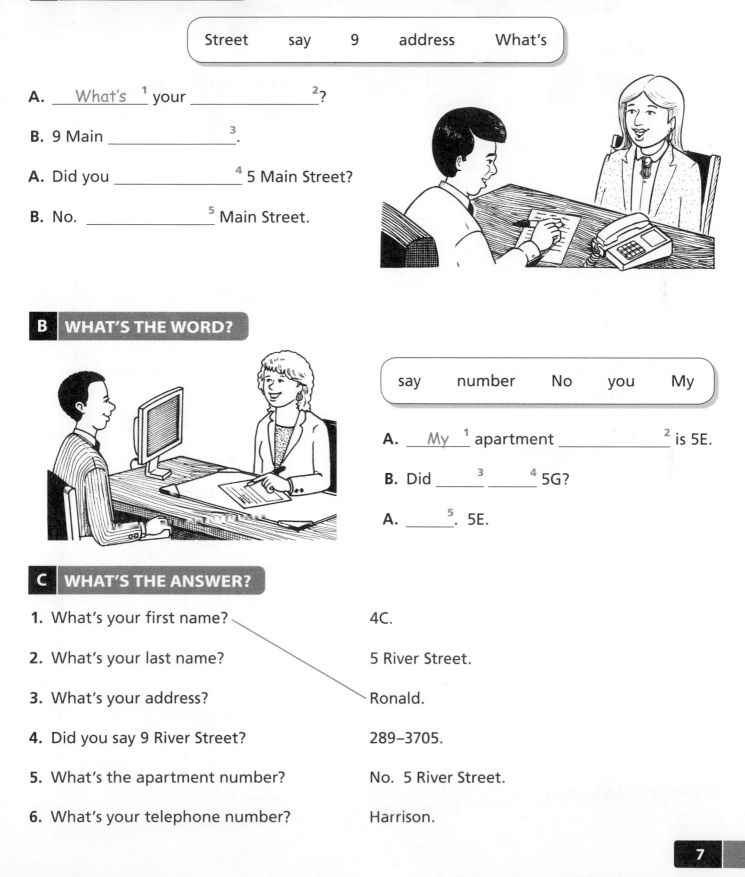

B WHAT'S THE WORD?

| say number No you My |

A. ___My___ [1] apartment _____[2] is 5E.

B. Did _____[3] _____[4] 5G?

A. _____[5]. 5E.

C WHAT'S THE ANSWER?

1. What's your first name?   4C.

2. What's your last name?   5 River Street.

3. What's your address?   Ronald.

4. Did you say 9 River Street?   289–3705.

5. What's the apartment number?   No. 5 River Street.

6. What's your telephone number?   Harrison.

Listen and write the information.

NAME	Bernardo ¹	²
	First	Last

NAME _____Bernardo___ 1 _____ 2
 First   Last

ADDRESS ___3___ _____ 4
 Number   Street   Apartment Number

 _____ 5 ___6___ _____ 7
 City   State   Zip Code

TELEPHONE ___8___ _____ 9
 Area Code   Number

E MY ADDRESS BOOK

Write the name, address, and telephone number of a friend in your address book.

Address Book

Name _____
 First   Last

Address _____
 Number   Street   Apartment Number

 _____
 City   State   Zip Code

Telephone Number _____
 Area Code   Number

UNIT **1** LESSON **5** FAMILY MEMBERS

A WHO ARE THEY?

mother	aunt	husband	nephew
brother	son	grandmother	granddaughter

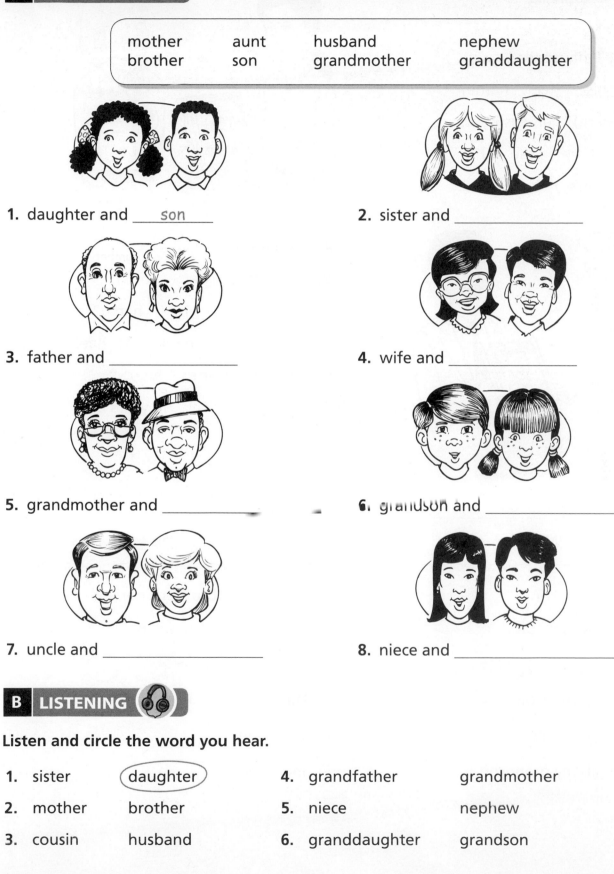

1. daughter and _____son_____

2. sister and _____

3. father and _____

4. wife and _____

5. grandmother and _____

6. grandson and _____

7. uncle and _____

8. niece and _____

B LISTENING

Listen and circle the word you hear.

1. sister   (daughter)   4. grandfather   grandmother

2. mother   brother   5. niece   nephew

3. cousin   husband   6. granddaughter   grandson

9

A WHICH WORD?

A. Who is this?

B. This is my ((daughter) wife).[1]

A. What's (his her)[2] name?

B. (His Her)[3] name is Rose.

A. How old is (he she)[4]?

B. (She's He's)[5] 9 years old.

A. Who is this?

B. This is my (sister son).[6]

A. What's (her his)[7] name?

B. (Her His)[8] name is Michael.

A. How old is (she he)[9] ?

B. (She's He's)[10] 10 years old.

B WHAT'S THE WORD?

old	Who	His	is	She's	your	This	He's

1. How old is your son?

   ___He's___ 4 years old.

2. How old is your daughter?

   _____ 9 years old.

3. Who is this?

   _____ is my grandson.

4. What's your brother's name?

   _____ name is Paul.

5. _____ is this?

   This _____ my niece.

6. How old is _____ sister?

   She's 2 years _____.

A WHAT'S THE WORD?

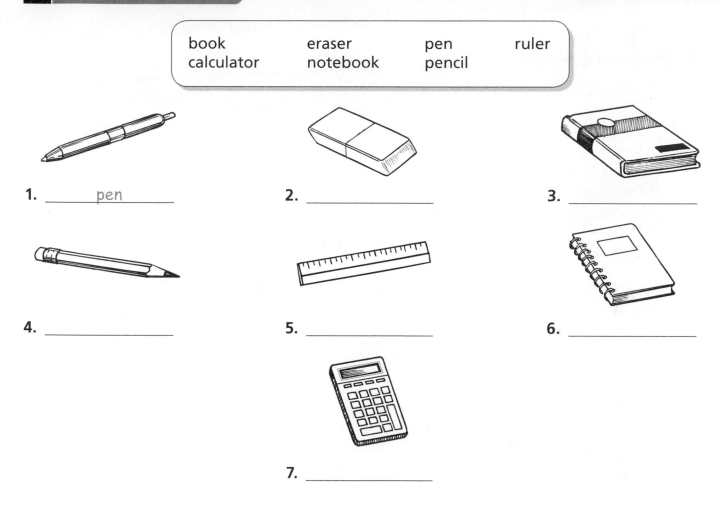

| book | eraser | pen | ruler |
| calculator | notebook | pencil | |

1. ____pen____

2. _____

3. _____

4. _____

5. _____

6. _____

7. _____

B LISTENING

Listen and circle the word you hear.

1. pen   (pencil)

2. ruler   eraser

3. notebook   book

4. calculator   eraser

5. pencil   pen

6. eraser   ruler

A MATCHING

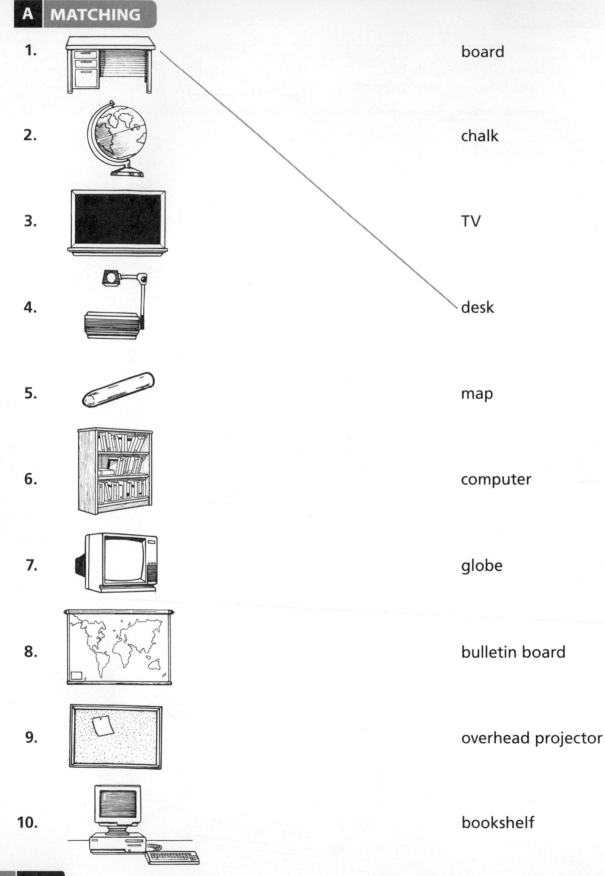

1.   board

2.   chalk

3.   TV

         desk

5.   map

6.   computer

7.   globe

8.   bulletin board

9.   overhead projector

10.   bookshelf

B WHERE ARE THEY?

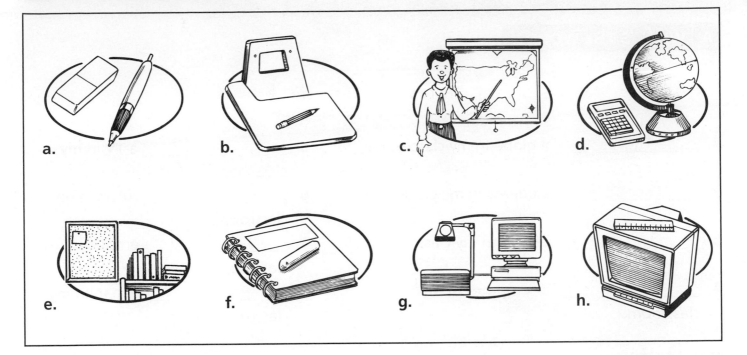

___c___ **1.** The teacher is next to the map.	_____ **5.** The calculator is next to the globe.
_____ **2.** The chalk is on the notebook.	_____ **6.** The eraser is next to the pen.
_____ **3.** The pencil is on the desk.	_____ **7.** The ruler is on the TV.
_____ **4.** The bulletin board is next to bookshelf.	_____ **8.** The overhead projector is next to the the computer.

C IN MY CLASSROOM

Put a check (✓) next to the things in your classroom.

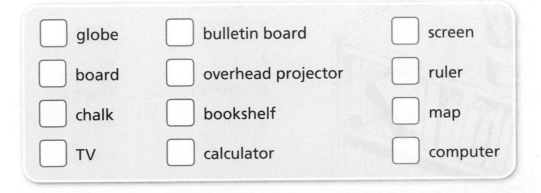

☐ globe	☐ bulletin board	☐ screen
☐ board	☐ overhead projector	☐ ruler
☐ chalk	☐ bookshelf	☐ map
☐ TV	☐ calculator	☐ computer

A WHAT'S THE WORD?

> There's   There are

1. _____There's_____ a globe in my classroom.

2. _____There are_____ students in my classroom.

3. _____ pencils in my classroom.

4. _____ a computer in my classroom.

5. _____ a TV in my classroom.

6. _____ rulers in my classroom.

7. _____ erasers in my classroom.

8. _____ a map in my classroom.

B MATCHING

1. There's a   calculators in my classroom.

2. There's an   computer in my classroom.

3. There's   my classroom.

4. There are   overhead projector in my classroom.

5. There's a bookshelf in   a globe in my classroom.

C LISTENING

Listen and circle the word you hear.

1. (pencils)   pens

2. desk   desks

3. a   an

4. There's   There are

5. on   in

6. an   are

A CHOOSE THE CORRECT ACTION

1. (a.) Open your book.
   b. Close your book.

2. a. Erase your name.
   b. Write your name.

3. a. Stand up.
   b. Sit down.

4. a. Raise your hand.
   b. Go to the board.

5. a. Write your name.
   b. Erase your name.

6. a. Take out your book.
   b. Put away your book.

B WHICH WORD?

1. (Go   (Stand)) up.

2. (Raise   Erase) your hand.

3. (Write   Go) to the board.

4. (Put away   Erase) your book.

5. (Stand   Sit) down.

15

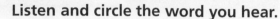

Listen and circle the word you hear.

1. (Open) Close   3. Put away   Take out   5. Write   Raise

2. Raise   Erase   4. Sit   Stand   6. Open   Go

D **YOU'RE THE TEACHER!**

You're the teacher. Write five instructions.

_____

_____

_____

_____

_____

E **LISTENING**

Listen and circle the correct answer.

1. (Yes, there is.)   No, there isn't.   5. Yes, there is.   No, there isn't.

2. Yes, there is.   No, there isn't.   6. Yes, there is.   No, there isn't.

3. Yes, there is.   No, there isn't.   7. Yes, there is.   No, there isn't.

4. Yes, there is.   No, there isn't.   8. Yes, there is.   No, there isn't.

UNIT 2 LESSON 5 NUMBERS IN THE CLASSROOM

STUDENT BOOK PAGE 28

A MATCHING

1. 14 — seventeen
2. 19 — fourteen
3. 17 — thirteen
4. 13 — nineteen
5. 15 — eleven
6. 11 — twelve
7. 18 — fifteen
8. 12 — eighteen

B LISTENING

Listen and circle the number you hear.

1. 15 (14)
2. 11 19
3. 17 12
4. 19 13
5. 15 16
6. 14 17

C NUMBER SEARCH

eleven	thirteen	fifteen	seventeen	nineteen
twelve	fourteen	sixteen	eighteen	

A	L	T	K	E	R	M	E	F	M	O	K	F
C	(E	L	E	V	E	N)	I	T	P	M	Z	O
T	H	R	T	E	F	N	E	W	E	L	E	U
I	F	E	T	H	I	R	T	E	E	N	L	R
N	I	R	T	H	F	R	T	L	E	N	E	T
E	F	I	F	T	T	L	E	V	C	U	V	E
I	T	R	I	E	E	E	S	E	V	E	N	E
G	S	I	X	T	E	E	N	R	O	T	T	N
H	F	Y	T	L	N	B	R	O	R	T	W	O
T	S	E	V	E	N	T	E	E	N	C	E	X
E	U	H	E	C	F	A	S	I	X	H	N	E
E	R	N	I	N	E	T	E	E	N	C	T	I
N	U	J	N	I	N	T	E	E	N	O	Y	O

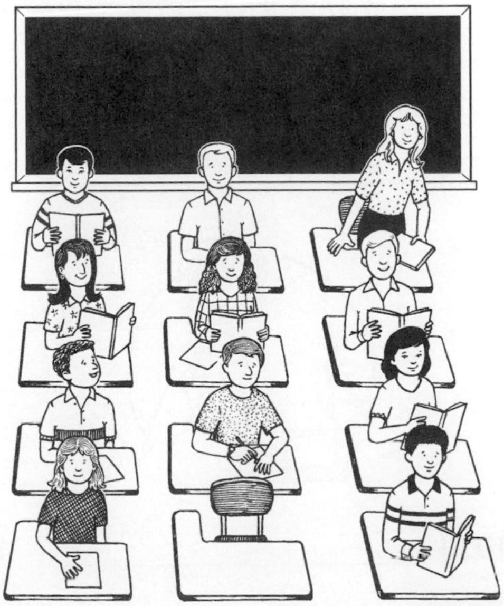

A EVERY DAY

brush my teeth	take a shower	get up	get undressed
get dressed	eat breakfast	watch TV	comb my hair
go to bed	come home	read	cook dinner

1. I _____watch TV_____.

2. I _____.

3. I _____.

4. I _____.

5. I _____.

6. I _____.

7. I _____.

8. I _____.

9. I _____.

10. I _____.

11. I _____.

12. I _____.

1. a. I watch TV.
   (b.) I read.

2. a. I comb my hair.
   b. I brush my teeth.

3. a. I go to school.
   b. I go to work.

4. a. I cook dinner.
   b. I eat dinner.

5. a. I get undressed.
   b. I get dressed.

6. a. I get up.
   b. I go to bed.

C **LISTENING**

Listen and write the number under the correct picture.

_____

_____

_____

_____

1

_____

_____

_____

_____

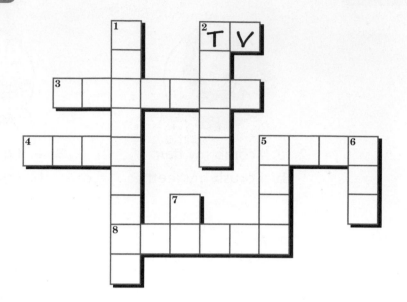

Across

2. Every day I watch _____.

3. Every day I get _____.

4. Every day I go to _____.

5. Every day I come _____.

8. Every day I take a _____.

Down

1. Every day I eat _____.

2. Every day I brush my _____.

5. Every day I comb my _____.

6. Every day I _____ lunch.

7. Every day I _____ to school.

E HOW ABOUT YOU?

Write about yourself.

Every day I _____

_____

_____

_____

_____ .

A CHOOSE THE CORRECT ACTIVITY

1. a. I'm cleaning.
   (b.) I'm making lunch.

2. a. I'm feeding the baby.
   b. I'm eating breakfast.

3. a. I'm washing the dishes.
   b. I'm doing the laundry.

4. a. I'm playing the guitar.
   b. I'm doing the laundry.

5. a. I'm studying.
   b. I'm exercising.

6. a. I'm listening to music.
   b. I'm ironing.

B LISTENING

Listen and write the number under the correct picture.

_____

_____

1

_____

_____

_____

C | WHICH WORD?

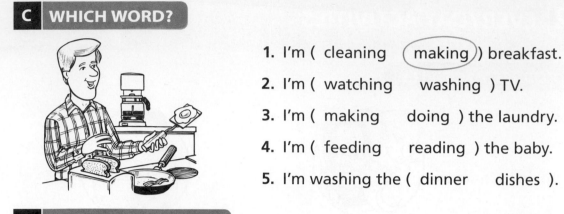

1. I'm (cleaning   (making)) breakfast.
2. I'm (watching   washing) TV.
3. I'm (making   doing) the laundry.
4. I'm (feeding   reading) the baby.
5. I'm washing the (dinner   dishes).

D | WHAT'S THE WORD?

| doing   making   feeding   watching   listening   playing |

1. I'm _____watching_____ TV.
2. I'm _____ the baby.
3. I'm _____ lunch.
4. I'm _____ the laundry.
5. I'm _____ the guitar.
6. I'm _____ to music.

E | WHAT ARE THEY SAYING?

Complete the conversation. Practice it with another student.

A. Hi. What are you doing?

B. I'm _____. How about you?

A. I'm _____.

A MATCHING

1. My father   cook dinner every day.
2. I'm   cooks dinner every day.
3. I   cooking dinner right now.

4. I   listens to music every day.
5. I'm   listen to music every day.
6. My brother   listening to music right now.

7. My sister   watch TV every day.
8. I   watching TV right now.
9. I'm   watches TV every day.

10. I'm   go to work every day.
11. My mother   going to work right now.
12. I   goes to work every day.

B EVERY DAY OR RIGHT NOW?

listen	brush	get	do	watch	play
listening	brushing	getting	doing	watching	playing
go	take	clean	eat	feed	wash
going	taking	cleaning	eating	feeding	washing

1. _____I clean_____ the house every day.
2. _____I'm eating_____ breakfast right now.
3. _____ the dishes every day.
4. _____ the guitar right now.
5. _____ to work every day.
6. _____ dressed right now.
7. _____ to music right now.
8. _____ my teeth every day.
9. _____ TV right now.
10. _____ the baby right now.
11. _____ the laundry every day.
12. _____ a shower every day.

Answer about yourself.

Yes, I do.   No, I don't.

1. Do you listen to music every day? _____

2. Do you make dinner every day? _____

3. Do you exercise every day? _____

4. Do you wash the dishes every day? _____

5. Do you clean the house every day? _____

6. Do you watch TV every day? _____

7. Do you eat lunch every day? _____

8. Do you study English every day? _____

D LISTENING 🎧

Listen and circle the sentence you hear.

1. a. I'm cleaning the house.
   b. I clean the house.

2. a. I'm making breakfast.
   b. I make breakfast.

3. a. I'm feeding the baby.
   b. I feed the baby.

4. a. I read.
   b. I'm reading.

5. a. I'm studying.
   b. I study.

6. a. I iron.
   b. I'm ironing.

7. a. I'm combing my hair.
   b. I comb my hair.

8. a. I eat lunch.
   b. I'm eating lunch.

9. a. I'm doing the laundry.
   b. I do the laundry.

10. a. I watch TV.
    b. I'm watching TV.

A **MATCHING**

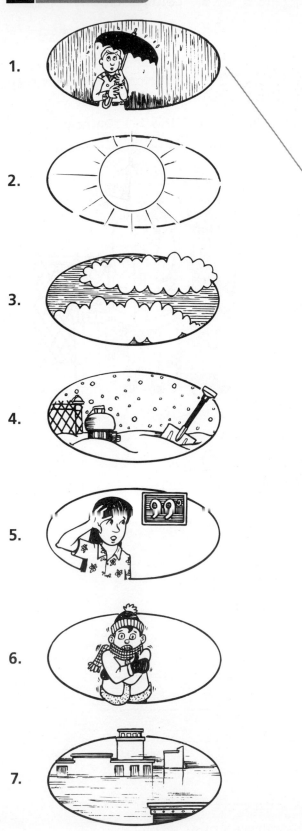

1.

2.

3.

4.

5.

6.

7.

It's cold.

It's sunny.

It's snowing.

It's raining.

It's foggy.

It's cloudy.

It's hot.

Listen and circle the word you hear.

1. (sunny)   cloudy   3. hot   cold   5. cold   cloudy

2. raining   snowing   4. foggy   sunny   6. hot   foggy

C WORD SEARCH

| cold | foggy | hot | snowing | cloudy | raining | sunny |

```
T  S  U  N  P  T  M  U  R  S  S  O
O  B (C  O  L  D) N  O  A  U  H  R
F  C  L  L  S  N  O  W  I  N  G  N
O  K  P  T  O  O  T  H  N  N  H  E
G  S  E  C  L  O  U  D  I  Y  T  E
G  N  A  Y  E  R  A  A  N  T  H  N
Y  O  R  U  H  E  F  C  G  V  E  T
O  U  A  S  O  A  O  H  A  O  K  S
U  W  C  I  T  S  C  L  O  U  D  Y
```

D WHAT'S THE WEATHER?

1. What's the weather in San Francisco?   It's _____ *foggy* _____.

2. What's the weather in New York?   It's _____.

3. What's the weather in Miami?   It's _____.

4. What's the weather in Denver?   It's _____.

5. What's the weather in Dallas?   It's _____.

6. What's the weather in Chicago?   It's _____.

7. What's the weather in Los Angeles?   It's _____.

A MATCHING

1. forty   66
2. thirty-five   70
3. seventy   40
4. sixty-six   22
5. twenty-two   35

6. fifty-four   90
7. one hundred   47
8. ninety   100
9. eighty-one   54
10. forty-seven   81

B WHAT'S THE NUMBER?

1. thirty   _30_
2. sixty   _____
3. fifty-three   _____
4. seventy-five   _____
5. forty-three   _____

6. eighty-nine   _____
7. ninety-one   _____
8. twenty-six   _____
9. fifty-eight   _____
10. sixty-two   _____

C WHAT'S THE WORD?

1. 20 _____twenty_____
2. 80 _____
3. 36 _____
4. 49 _____
5. 57 _____

6. 63 _____
7. 78 _____
8. 84 _____
9. 92 _____
10. 21 _____

D LISTENING

Listen and circle the number you hear.

1. 50   (60)
2. 21   31
3. 44   54

4. 72   27
5. 65   69
6. 54   43

7. 99   89
8. 84   44
9. 53   33

UNITS 1–3 CHECK-UP TEST

A MATCHING

1. What's the weather?   It's on the bookshelf.

2. What are you doing?   Yes, it is.

3. Where's the globe?   It's raining.

4. Who is this?   He's ten years old.

5. How old is your son?   I'm cooking.

6. Is this your notebook?   This is my sister.

B WHICH WORD?

1. This is my daughter. (He's   She's) seven years old.

2. There's (a   an) overhead projector in my classroom.

3. Raise your (hand   name).

4. I take a (shower   breakfast) every day.

5. Right now I'm (read   reading).

6. My (apartment   telephone) number is 5C.

7. There are (desk   globes) in my classroom.

8. I (watch   watching) TV every day.

C LISTENING

Listen and circle the words you hear.

1. I'm   My   4. husband   cousin

2. computer   calculator   5. open   close

3. 768–3569   768–3965   6. cleaning   reading

A   WHAT'S THE NUMBER?

eighty	fifty	nineteen	seventy	sixty	thirty-three
eleven	forty	one hundred	sixteen	thirteen	twenty

70 ___seventy___   16 _____   50 _____

20 _____   100 _____   40 _____

13 _____   33 _____   19 _____

80 _____   11 _____   60 _____

B   WHAT'S THE ANSWER?

1. How much is five plus four?   thirty-four

2. How much is three plus two?   fifty

3. How much is eight plus seven?   nine

4. How much is twenty plus fourteen?   fifteen

5. How much is forty plus ten?   five

C   WHAT'S THE ORDER?

Put the numbers in the correct order.

1. __2__ fifteen   3. _____ seventy-six

   __3__ fifty   _____ sixty-three

   __1__ five   _____ thirty-four

2. _____ nineteen   4. _____ thirty-nine

   _____ ninety-nine   _____ ninety-nine

   _____ nine   _____ forty-nine

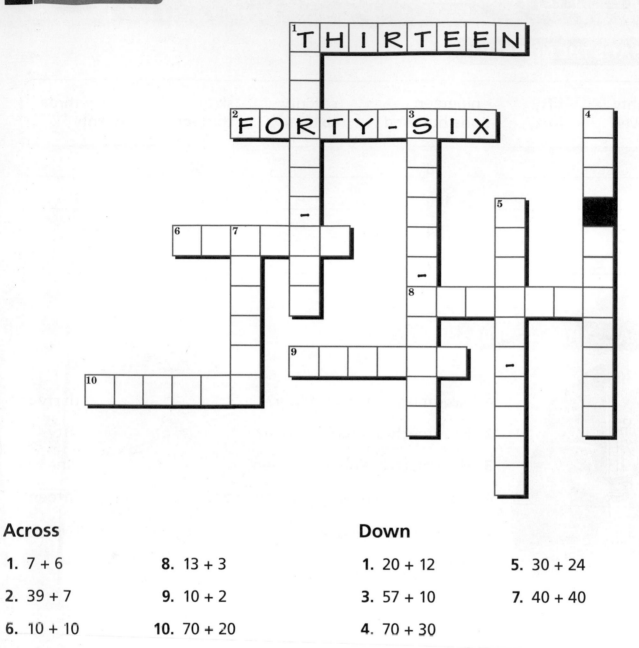

Across

1. 7 + 6

2. 39 + 7

6. 10 + 10

8. 13 + 3

9. 10 + 2

10. 70 + 20

Down

1. 20 + 12

3. 57 + 10

4. 70 + 30

5. 30 + 24

7. 40 + 40

E LISTENING

Listen and circle the number you hear.

1. (1355 Main Street)   3055 Main Street

2. 1697 Main Street   697 Main Street

3. 3419 River Street   3490 River Street

4. 1474 Center Street   4174 Center Street

5. 1790 Pine Street   1719 Pine Street

6. Apartment 509   Apartment 905

7. Apartment 140   Apartment 114

8. Room 880   Room 818

9. Room 223   Room 232

10. Room 110   Room 101

A MATCHING

1. It's eight fifteen.

2. It's four o'clock.

3. It's six thirty.

4. It's three forty-five.

5. It's twelve o'clock.

6. It's two fifteen.

7. It's seven thirty.

8. It's four forty-five.

9. It's eight thirty.

10. It's five o'clock.

B LISTENING

Listen and put a check (✓) under the time you hear.

1. _____   ___✓___

2. _____   _____

3. _____   _____

4. _____   _____

5. _____   _____

6. _____   _____

A DAYS OF THE WEEK WORD SEARCH

Sunday	Monday	Tuesday	Wednesday	Thursday	Friday	Saturday

```
S  U  N  D  A  Y  I  M  E  F  T  O  K  L  A
T  H  U  R  D  A  Y  M  S  O  U  D  A  Y  W
M  O  N  D  U  Y  M  O  U  E  E  D  A  Y  T
L  O  T  O  N  R  Y  N  D  S  S  T  D  A  Y
W  E  N  S  D  T  N  D  A  V  D  W  S  G  M
C  D  P  D  S  H  I  A  Y  I  A  E  A  S  O
H  A  Z  O  T  U  N  Y  D  E  Y  D  T  A  D
B  Y  B  Y  H  R  E  R  T  R  O  N  O  T  A
W  E  D  N  E  S  D  A  Y  O  R  E  R  U  Y
S  A  T  O  R  D  A  Y  E  F  F  S  D  R  E
F  A  T  U  S  A  F  A  D  I  R  D  A  D  L
F  R  I  A  D  Y  H  U  A  S  I  A  Y  A  N
P  S  U  D  A  Y  I  O  F  R  I  D  A  Y  L
T  U  E  D  Y  Y  N  A  Y  P  A  E  C  B  N
W  E  D  N  D  A  Y  G  R  I  Y  Z  M  A  H
```

B WHAT'S THE ORDER?

Put the days of the week in the correct order.

_____ Wednesday	_____ Tuesday
_____ Saturday	___1___ Sunday
_____ Monday	_____ Thursday
_____ Friday	

C LISTENING

Listen and circle the word you hear.

1. Thursday   (Tuesday)
2. Friday   Wednesday
3. 5:30   9:30

4. Tuesday   Thursday
5. 2:15   4:15
6. Saturday   Sunday

1. T H U _R_ S _D_ A Y

3. M __ __ N D A __

5. __ __ I D A Y

2. S __ __ T __ __ R D A Y

4. T U __ __ __ __ D A Y

6. W __ __ D N E __ __ D A Y

E | WHAT'S THE DAY?

| Sunday | Monday | Tuesday | Wednesday | Thursday | Friday | Saturday |

1. I clean on _____Tuesday_____.

5. I do the laundry on _____.

2. I exercise on _____.

6. I play basketball on _____.

3. I iron on _____.

7. I relax on _____.

4. I watch TV on _____.

F | WHAT DO YOU DO EVERY DAY?

Write about yourself.

I _____ on _____.

I _____ on _____.

I _____ on _____.

I _____ on _____.

I _____ on _____.

I _____ on _____.

I _____ on _____.

A WHICH FLOOR?

1. I live on the tenth floor.

1st
(10th)

3. We live on the second floor.

2nd

12th

5. I live on the fortieth floor.

4th

40th

7. I live on the thirteenth floor.

3rd

13th

2. I live on the sixteenth floor.

6th

16th

4. I live on the seventy-seventh floor.

17th

77th

6. We live on the fifteenth floor.

15th

50th

8. We live on the eightieth floor.

8th

80th

B WHAT'S THE NUMBER?

fourth	first	twelfth	sixth	ninetieth
ninth	eighth	nineteenth	third	

3rd _____third_____   **6th** _____   **19th** _____

9th _____   **90th** _____   **8th** _____

4th _____   **12th** _____   **1st** _____

LISTENING 🎧

Listen and circle the number you hear.

1.	70th	(17th)	**5.**	3rd	33rd	**9.**	40th	14th
2.	6th	5th	**6.**	8th	80th	**10.**	16th	66th
3.	11th	12th	**7.**	47th	42nd	**11.**	19th	9th
4.	1st	5th	**8.**	15th	50th	**12.**	45th	54th

D **CROSSWORD**

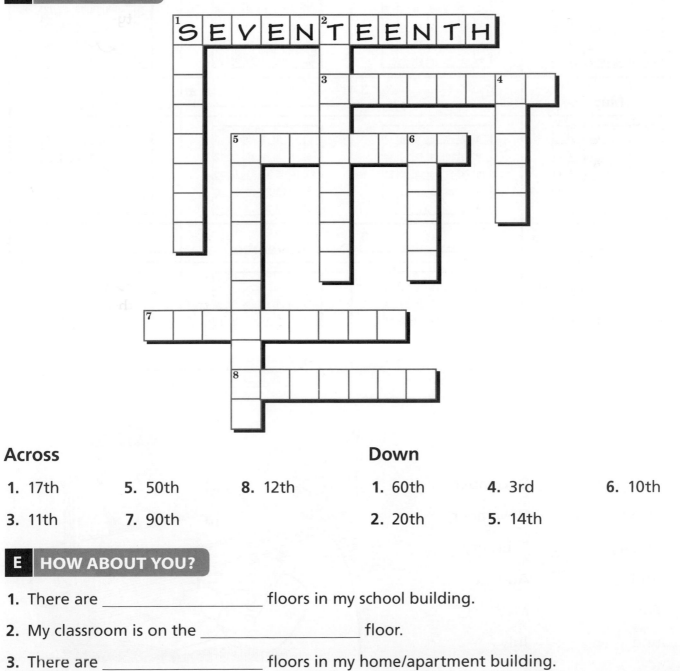

S E V E N T E E N T H

Across

1. 17th	**5.** 50th	**8.** 12th
3. 11th	**7.** 90th	

Down

1. 60th	**4.** 3rd	**6.** 10th
2. 20th	**5.** 14th	

E **HOW ABOUT YOU?**

1. There are _____ floors in my school building.

2. My classroom is on the _____ floor.

3. There are _____ floors in my home/apartment building.

4. I live on the _____ floor.

A WHAT'S THE MONTH?

October   March   December   July   September   January   June

| _January_ **1** | **February** | _____ **2** | **April** |

1 2 3 4		1	1 2 3 4 5
5 6 7 8 9 10 11	2 3 4 5 6 7 8	2 3 4 5 6 7 8	6 7 8 9 10 11 12
12 13 14 15 16 17 18	9 10 11 12 13 14 15	9 10 11 12 13 14 15	13 14 15 16 17 18 19
19 20 21 22 23 24 25	16 17 18 19 20 21 22	16 17 18 19 20 21 22	20 21 22 23 24 25 26
26 27 28 29 30 31	23 24 25 26 27 28	23/30 24/31 25 26 27 28 29	27 28 29 30

| **May** | _____ **3** | _____ **4** | **August** |

1 2 3	1 2 3 4 5 6 7	1 2 3 4 5	1 2
4 5 6 7 8 9 10	8 9 10 11 12 13 14	6 7 8 9 10 11 12	3 4 5 6 7 8 9
11 12 13 14 15 16 17	15 16 17 18 19 20 21	13 14 15 16 17 18 19	10 11 12 13 14 15 16
18 19 20 21 22 23 24	22 23 24 25 26 27 28	20 21 22 23 24 25 26	17 18 19 20 21 22 23
25 26 27 28 29 30 31	29 30	27 28 29 30 31	24/31 25 26 27 28 29 30

| _____ **5** | _____ **6** | **November** | _____ **7** |

1 2 3 4 5 6	1 2 3 4	1	1 2 3 4 5 6
7 8 9 10 11 12 13	5 6 7 8 9 10 11	2 3 4 5 6 7 8	7 8 9 10 11 12 13
14 15 16 17 18 19 20	12 13 14 15 16 17 18	9 10 11 12 13 14 15	14 15 16 17 18 19 20
21 22 23 24 25 26 27	19 20 21 22 23 24 25	16 17 18 19 20 21 22	21 22 23 24 25 26 27
28 29 30	26 27 28 29 30 31	23/30 24 25 26 27 28 29	28 29 30 31

B LISTENING

Listen and circle the month you hear.

1. (September)   December
2. October   November
3. January   February
4. April   August
5. March   May
6. June   July

C WHAT'S THE ORDER?

_____ February

_____ December

_____ October

_____ September

_____ August

_____ April

_____ July

_____ November

_____ June

___1___ January

_____ March

_____ May

D MATCHING

1. What day is it today?   It's May.

2. What month is it?   It's two fifteen.

3. What's today's date?   It's Tuesday.

4. What time is it?   It's December 10, 2012.

E WHAT'S THE ANSWER?

1. What day is it today? _____

2. What month is it?   _____

3. What's today's date?   _____

4. What time is it now?   _____

F LISTENING

Listen and circle the correct answer.

1. December 19th   November 9th

2. August 1st   August 3rd

3. June 7, 2012   June 11, 2012

4. January 15, 2012   January 5, 2012

5. from 5 to 9   from 9 to 5

6. from 8:30 to 3   from 8 to 3:30

A WHAT'S THE COIN?

| penny | nickel | dime | quarter | half dollar |

1. ___nickel___   2. _____   3. _____   4. _____   5. _____

B MATCHING

1. quarter $.01
2. dime $.25
3. penny $.10

4. nickel   50¢
5. half dollar   25¢
6. quarter   5¢

C HOW MUCH MONEY?

1. ___fifteen dollars___

2. _____

3. _____

4. _____

5. _____

6. _____

D MATCHING

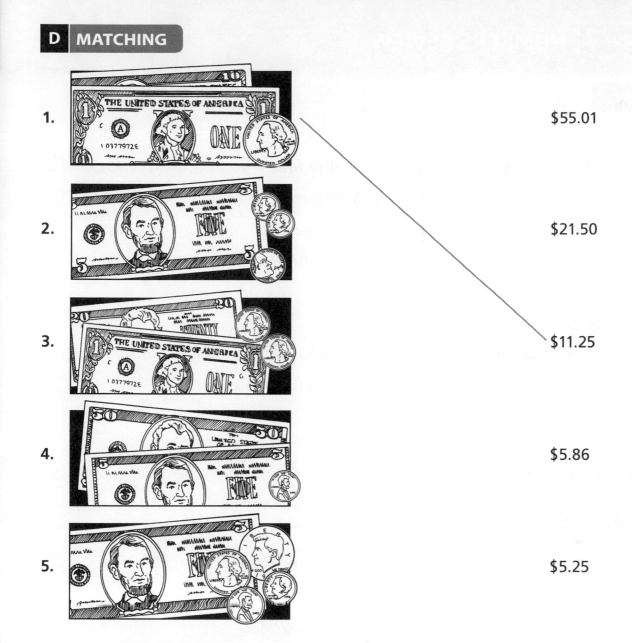

1. $55.01

2. $21.50

3. $11.25

4. $5.86

5. $5.25

E WHICH ONE DOESN'T BELONG?

1.	50¢	fifteen cents	$.50	half dollar
2.	twenty-five cents	$.25	quarter	$25
3.	dime	10¢	$10	$.10
4.	1¢	nickel	one cent	$.01
5.	$.05	50¢	nickel	five cents
6.	$1.00	one dollar	4 quarters	$.10
7.	$20.00	twenty dollars	2 ten-dollar bills	$.20

A MATCHING

1. six	60th	6. forty-fifth	$15.50
2. sixteenth	6	7. fifty-four	1515
3. sixty	1660	8. fifteen fifteen	45th
4. sixtieth	16th	9. fifteen fifty	5:15
5. sixteen sixty	60	10. five fifteen	54

B WHICH WORD?

1. Nine plus five is (fourteenth (fourteen)).

2. I live at (thirty   thirtieth) Main Street.

3. My English class is in Room (245   2:45).

4. I live on the (three   third) floor.

5. Can you come in today at (9:30 $9.30)?

6. April is the (four   fourth) month of the year.

7. It's (eleven   eleventh) o'clock.

8. Today's date is November (ten   tenth).

C WHICH ONE DOESN'T BELONG?

1. twenty   forty-five   (sixteenth)   eighty-nine

2. $.05   50¢   nickel   5:00

3. six thirty $6.45   4:00   nine o'clock

4. seventh   first   seven   second

5. 7:00   nine o'clock   3:15   twelve o'clock

D LISTENING

Listen and circle the correct numbers.

1. (28)	82	4. 1st	3rd	7. $2.00	2:00
2. 3:20	320	5. 14th	40th	8. 5 to 9	9 to 5
3. 1:30	10:30	6. 12th	11th	9. 6th	fifth

A WHAT'S THE WORD?

balcony	bedroom	kitchen	patio
bathroom	dining room	living room	

1. _____living room_____

2. _____

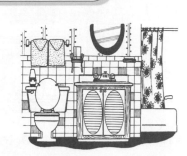

3. _____

4. _____

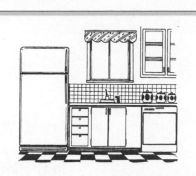

5. _____

6. _____

7. _____

B LISTENING

Listen and circle the word you hear.

1. kitchen   (living room)

2. bathroom   balcony

3. living room   dining room

4. balcony   patio

5. bedroom   bathroom

6. living room   kitchen

41

A WHAT'S THE WORD?

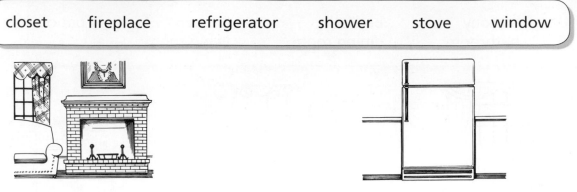

closet   fireplace   refrigerator   shower   stove   window

1. This is a very nice apartment.

There's a ___fireplace___ in the living room.

2. There's a nice _____
in the kitchen.

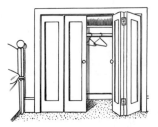

3. There's also a _____
in the kitchen.

4. There's a _____ in
the bedroom.

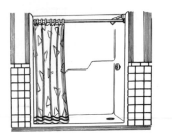

5. There's a _____ in the
bathroom.

6. There's also a _____
in the bathroom.

B WHICH WORD?

1. There's a (fireplace   (shower)) in the bathroom.

2. There's a (refrigerator   closet) in the bedroom.

3. There's a (stove   shower) in the kitchen.

4. There's a (shower   fireplace) in the living room.

bathroom   kitchen   stove   closet   window   fireplace   shower   bedroom

```
D  E  S  H  L  K  S (C  L  O  S  E  T) P
K  I  T  C  H  E  N  A  G  L  U  V  P  W
L  I  O  E  N  R  Y  A  H  L  U  V  A  B
E  N  V  E  I  F  I  R  E  P  L  A  C  E
C  I  E  T  Z  P  I  L  G  K  C  U  R  D
H  S  Z  O  P  A  N  E  R  E  B  E  W  R
C  H  B  Y  B  A  T  H  R  O  O  M  O  O
W  O  S  H  O  W  R  B  R  O  R  T  R  O
A  W  O  N  A  S  C  N  O  F  C  C  T  M
F  E  U  H  B  C  F  A  S  I  L  H  T  E
Q  R  R  C  D  V  B  E  D  R  M  M  P  I
P  S  U  J  O  W  I  F  E  E  S  T  Y  O
W  I  N  D  O  W  N  A  Y  P  E  E  C  B
T  E  R  O  B  C  K  G  R  I  T  Z  M  A
```

D LISTENING

Listen and write the number under the correct picture.

_____

1

_____

_____

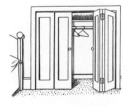
_____

_____

_____

_____

_____

A MATCHING

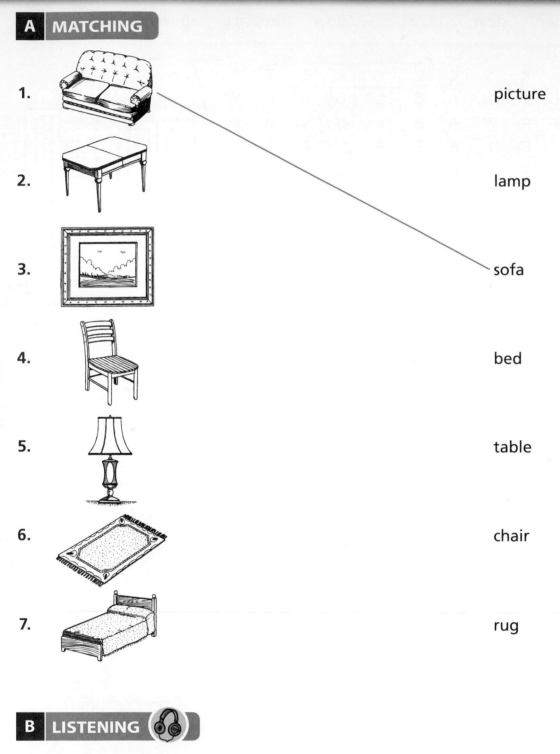

1.

picture

2.

lamp

3.

sofa

4.

bed

5.

table

6.

chair

7.

rug

B LISTENING

Listen and circle the word you hear.

1. bedroom (bed)   3. living room   kitchen   5. dining room   table

2. sofa   stove   4. picture   refrigerator   6. balcony   lamp

Circle the correct answer.

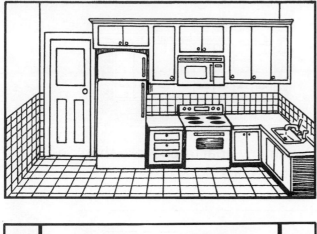

1. Is there a stove in the kitchen? (Yes, there is.) No, there isn't.

2. Is there a bed in the bedroom? Yes, there is. No, there isn't.

3. Is there a fireplace in the living room? Yes, there is. No, there isn't.

4. Is there a fireplace in the bedroom? Yes, there is. No, there isn't.

5. Is there a picture in the dining room? Yes, there is. No, there isn't.

6. Is there a rug in the living room? Yes, there is. No, there isn't.

7. Is there a window in the kitchen? Yes, there is. No, there isn't.

8. Is there a chair in the living room? Yes, there is. No, there isn't.

9. Is there a table in the kitchen? Yes, there is. No, there isn't.

10. Is there a lamp in the living room? Yes, there is. No, there isn't.

11. Is there a bookshelf in the living room? Yes, there is. No, there isn't.

A WHAT'S THE ANSWER?

1. How many floors are there in the building?

There are four floors.

2. How many apartments are there in the building?

_____

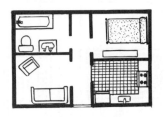

3. How many rooms are there in the apartment?

_____

4. How many closets are there in the bedroom?

_____

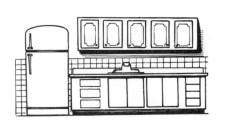

5. How many cabinets are there in the kitchen?

_____

6. How many windows are there in the living room?

_____

B WHICH WORD?

1. My apartment building is on (Ten　(Tenth)) Street.

2. There are (four　fourth) floors in the building.

3. My apartment is on the (three　third) floor.

4. There are (two　twelfth) closets in my bedroom.

A WHAT'S THE WORD?

bakery	bus station	drug store	grocery store	library
bank	clinic	gas station	laundromat	

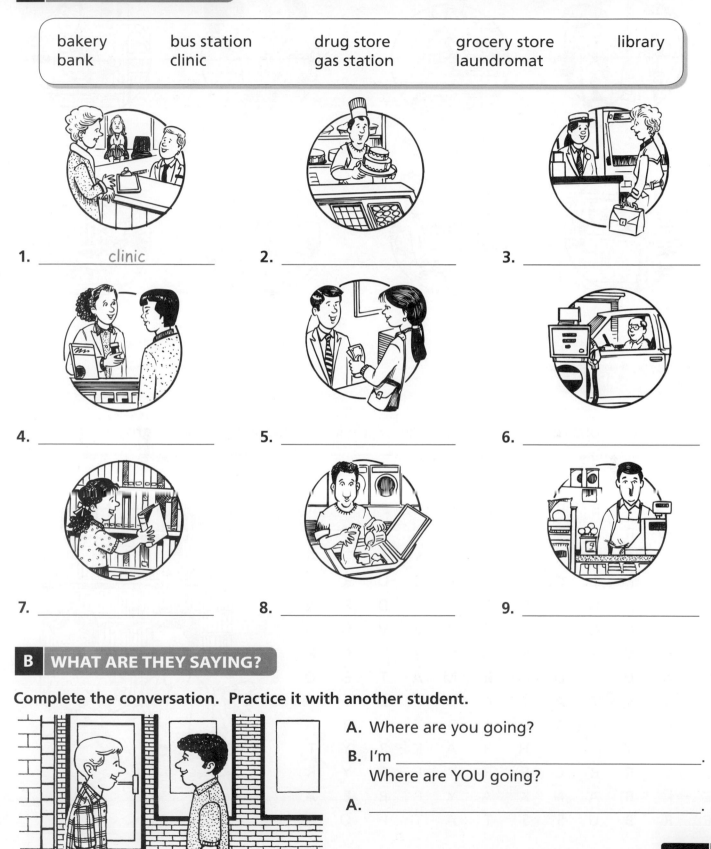

1. _____clinic_____ 2. _____ 3. _____

4. _____ 5. _____ 6. _____

7. _____ 8. _____ 9. _____

B WHAT ARE THEY SAYING?

Complete the conversation. Practice it with another student.

A. Where are you going?

B. I'm _____.
Where are YOU going?

A. _____.

C LISTENING

Listen and put a check (✓) under the place you hear.

1. _____   ✓_____   2. _____   _____

3. _____   _____   4. _____   _____

D WORD SEARCH

| library | bus station | laundromat | clinic | bakery | bank | grocery store |

```
I  B  R  B  R  I  M  E  F  M  O  K
H  L  I  B  R  A  R  Y  S  P  O  R
G  W  R  T  T  M  B  A  N  S  D  L
R  T  E  A  R  Y  A  N  S  A  T  A
O  C  L  T  C  L  N  I  C  D  R  U
C  L  I  N  I  C  R  A  I  D  E  N
E  Z  O  O  A  N  E  Y  E  V  D  D
R  B  Y  N  G  R  O  C  R  Y  N  R
Y  A  U  N  D  O  R  M  A  T  E  O
S  K  S  T  A  T  I  O  F  B  S  M
T  E  E  S  A  R  T  S  T  A  R  A
O  R  Y  T  N  H  B  A  K  R  Y  T
R  Y  R  R  C  E  R  Y  E  E  Y  R
E  I  B  A  N  K  A  Y  P  R  E  A
E  R  B  U  S  S  T  A  T  I  O  N
```

A MATCHING

_____ **1.** The park is over there.

_____ **2.** The supermarket is over there.

_____ **3.** The restaurant is over there.

_____ **4.** The hospital is over there.

_____ **5.** The movie theater is over there.

_____ **6.** The shopping mall is over there.

_____ **7.** The department store is over there.

_____ **8.** The zoo is over there.

_____ **9.** The post office is over there.

_____ **10.** The train station is over there.

B WHAT ARE THEY SAYING?

Complete the conversation. Practice it with another student.

A. Where are you going?

B. I'm _____.
Where are YOU going?

A. _____.

WHICH PLACE DOESN'T BELONG?

1. supermarket   grocery store   movie theater

2. train station   shopping mall   bus station

3. bank   grocery store   bakery

4. hospital   park   clinic

5. shopping mall   department store   post office

D **LISTENING**

Listen and put a check (✓) under the two places you hear.

1. _____✓_____   _____   _____✓_____

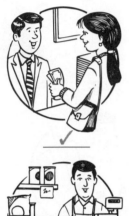

2. _____   _____   _____

3. _____   _____   _____

4. _____   _____   _____

A WHERE ARE THEY?

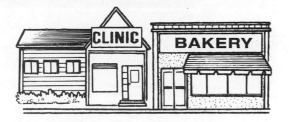

1. (a.) The clinic is next to the bakery.
  b. The clinic is across from the bakery.

2. a. The post office is across from the park.
  b. The post office is next to the park.

3. a. The hospital is on Pine Street.
  b. The hospital is on Main Street.

4. a. The restaurant is next to the zoo.
  b. The restaurant is between the zoo.

5. a. The library is next to the bank.
  b. The library is across from the bank.

6. a. The school is on Central Avenue.
  b. The school is on Center Street.

7. a. The department store is between the movie theater and the restaurant.
  b. The movie theater is between the department store and the restaurant.

1. The drug store is (in   (on)) Pine Street.

2. The supermarket is (next to   across from) the park.

3. The school is (next to   across from) the library.

4. The clinic is (across from   between)
   the restaurant and the bus station.

5. The shopping mall is (on   next to)
   Maple Street.

6. The gas station is (between   across from)
   the laundromat.

C | **LISTENING**

Listen and write the number under the correct picture.

_____

_____

_____

_____

_____

1

A WHAT'S THE WORD?

next to   on   across from   between

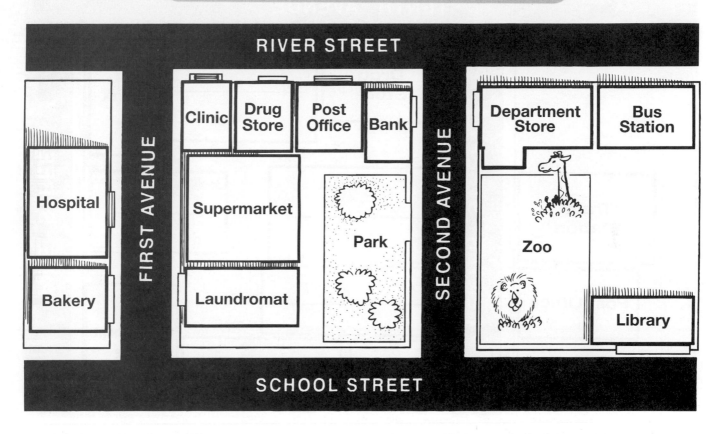

1. There's a supermarket on First Avenue, _____ across from _____ the hospital.

2. There's a zoo on Second Avenue, _____ the department store.

3. There's a department store _____ Second Avenue, across from the bank.

4. There's a post office on River Street, _____ the drug store and the bank.

5. There's a laundromat on First Avenue, _____ the supermarket.

6. There's a hospital _____ First Avenue, next to the bakery.

7. There's a drug store on River Street, _____ the clinic and the post office.

8. There's a park on Second Avenue, _____ the zoo.

Listen and write the names of the places on the map.

Bakery   Library   Movie Theater   Park   Restaurant   Shopping Mall

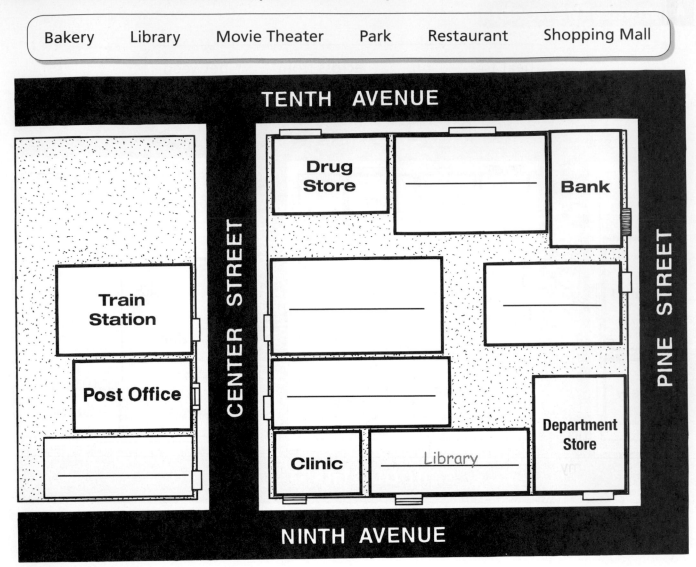

TENTH AVENUE

Drug Store

Bank

_____

CENTER STREET

PINE STREET

Train Station

_____

Post Office

_____

Department Store

Clinic

Library _____

_____

NINTH AVENUE

C WHICH WORD?

1. There's a movie theater on (Eleven   (Eleventh)) Street.

2. There are (three   third) clinics in my neighborhood.

3. The post office is on Sixty- (Five   Sixth) Street.

4. Is there a gas station on (Second   Seven) Avenue?

5. There's a very nice park on (Twelve   Thirteenth) Street.

6. There are (fourth   four) laundromats on (Eight   Eighth) Avenue.

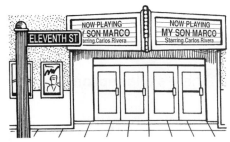

ELEVENTH ST

NOW PLAYING
MY SON MARCO
Starring Carlos Rivera

NOW PLAYING
MY SON MARCO
Starring Carlos Rivera

A MATCHING

1. What month is it?   It's Saturday.

2. What day is it?   It's on State Street.

3. What time is it?   It's September.

4. Where's the bank?   Yes, there is.

5. Is there a stove in the kitchen?   It's seven thirty.

B WHAT'S THE WORD?

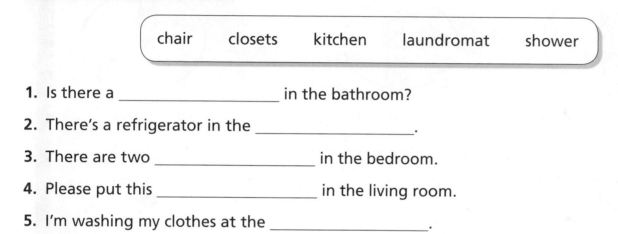

chair   closets   kitchen   laundromat   shower

1. Is there a _____ in the bathroom?

2. There's a refrigerator in the _____.

3. There are two _____ in the bedroom.

4. Please put this _____ in the living room.

5. I'm washing my clothes at the _____.

C WHICH WORD?

1. We live on the (second   seven) floor.

2. There's a (patio   stove) in the kitchen.

3. The bank is (across from   between) the park.

4. There's a bus station on (the laundromat   Main Street).

D LISTENING

Listen and circle the words you hear.

1. 1915   1519   4. fortieth   fourth

2. 11:30   7:30   5. Tuesday   Thursday

3. bus station   gas station   6. dining room   living room

A CHOOSE

1. He's ((young)   old).   2. She's (young   old).   3. He's (young   middle-aged).

4. She's (short   tall).   5. He's (short   tall).   6. She's (tall   average height).

B WHICH WORD?

1. He isn't tall. He's (young   (short)).

2. She isn't young. She's (tall   old).

3. I'm not old. I'm (short   young).

4. They aren't short. They're (middle-aged   tall).

5. We aren't young, and we aren't old. We're (average height   middle-aged).

6. I'm not tall, and I'm not short. I'm (average height   young).

C LISTENING

Listen and circle the word you hear.

1. old   (young)   3. young   short   5. average height   middle-aged

2. tall   old   4. middle-aged   average height   6. short   old

A WHICH WORD?

1. He has (black   blue) hair.

2. She has (green   blond) hair.

3. He has (white   blue) eyes.

4. She (have   has) black hair.

5. They (have   has) green eyes.

6. I (have   has) brown hair and brown eyes.

7. She has (gray   green) hair and (blue   blond) eyes.

B MISSING LETTERS

black	brown	green	white
blue	gray	red	

1. I have b l u e eyes.

2. My mother has ___ ___ ___ c ___ hair.

3. My sisters have ___ ___ ___ hair and ___ ___ o ___ ___ eyes.

4. My brother has ___ ___ ___ ___ n eyes.

5. My grandfather has ___ ___ ___ t ___ hair.

6. My grandmother has blue eyes and ___ ___ ___ ___ hair.

C LISTENING

Listen and circle the word you hear.

1. black   brown   4. green   white

2. gray   green   5. blond   brown

3. blue   black   6. brown   black

D | WHAT'S THE WORD?

black	curly	hair	height	short	straight	tall

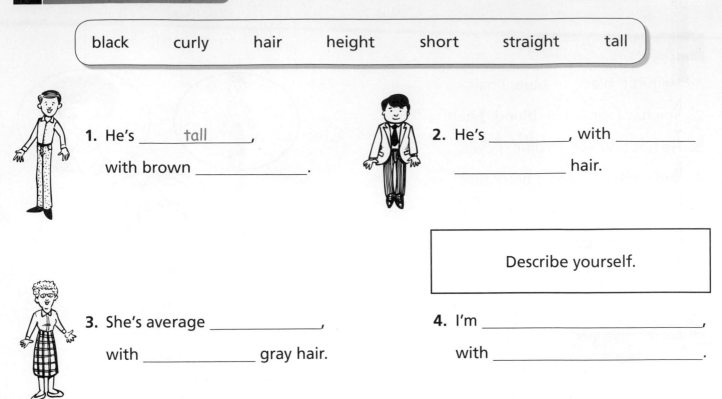

1. He's _____tall_____, with brown _____.

2. He's _____, with _____ _____ hair.

Describe yourself.

3. She's average _____, with _____ gray hair.

4. I'm _____, with _____.

E | LISTENING

Listen and put a check (✓) under the correct person.

1. _____   ____✓____   2. _____   _____   3. _____   _____

4. _____   _____   5. _____   _____   6. _____   _____

A MATCHING

1. My brother isn't married.
2. This is my cousin and his wife.
3. My aunt Helen isn't married now.
4. I'm not married now.

I'm divorced.

She's widowed.

He's single.

They're married.

B WHAT'S THE WORD?

afraid   angry   happy   hungry   sad   sick   thirsty   tired

1. I'm _____hungry_____.

2. I'm _____.

3. I'm _____.

4. I'm _____.

5. I'm _____.

6. I'm _____.

7. I'm _____.

8. I'm _____.

Listen and put a check (✓) under the correct picture.

1. _____   ✓ _____   2. _____   _____

3. _____   _____   4. _____   _____

D WORD SEARCH

afraid   angry   happy   hungry   married   sad   sick   single   thirsty   tired   upset

```
L  I  B  R  D  R  I  S  I  K  M  O  K  S
D  H  G  R  E  W  E  R  T  M  S  O  R  I
S  A  F  R  A  I  D  U  A  N  S  D  A  C
R  H  U  N  G  B  W  P  N  P  C  E  E  K
T  U  C  L  R  T  I  R  H  D  P  Y  G  G
H  N  P  T  N  I  B  E  A  N  G  R  Y  C
U  G  Z  O  G  F  Y  A  P  D  V  D  Y  U
N  R  B  Y  S  A  D  S  P  O  R  T  R  P
R  Y  A  U  Y  E  R  M  Y  U  T  I  Y  S
Y  S  T  H  A  G  R  I  O  F  B  R  S  E
F  B  S  M  A  R  R  I  E  D  S  E  I  T
Q  D  A  Y  E  N  H  U  A  S  K  D  O  S
S  I  N  G  L  E  R  R  Y  E  H  K  R  O
A  L  I  N  R  Y  N  T  H  I  R  S  T  Y
D  I  R  O  D  H  M  A  R  T  Y  O  R  E
```

A MATCHING

1. I'm from   Haitian.

   I speak   Haiti.

2. I'm from   Vietnamese.

   I speak   Vietnam.

3. I'm from   Japan.

   I speak   Japanese.

4. I'm from   Greek.

   I speak   Greece.

5. I'm from   Portuguese.

   I speak   Brazil.

6. I'm from   China.

   I speak   Chinese.

7. I'm from   Spanish.

   I speak   Mexico.

8. I'm from   Korean.

   I speak   Korea.

9. I'm from   Russia.

   I speak   Russian.

10. I'm from   Arabic.

    I speak   Morocco.

B WHICH WORD?

1. I'm from (Spanish   (Mexico)).

2. I speak (Russia   Russian).

3. My grandfather is from (Brazil   Portuguese).

4. It's raining today in (Japanese   Japan).

5. My teacher is from (Greek   Greece). She speaks (Greece   Greek).

C LISTENING

Listen and circle the word you hear.

1. (Mexico)   Morocco   4. Japan   Japanese   7. Vietnamese   Vietnam

2. Haiti   Haitian   5. Korea   Korean   8. Mexico   Brazil

3. China   Chinese   6. Russian   Russia   9. Greek   Greece

A **WHAT'S THE WORD?**

| height | middle-aged | pounds | short | weight | years | young |

1. She's twenty-five _____*years*_____ old.

2. He's thin. He weighs 75 _____.

3. She's 5 feet tall. She's _____.

4. He's forty years old. He isn't young, and he isn't old. He's _____.

5. He's average _____. He weighs 150 pounds.

6. He's _____. He's 4 years old.

7. She's average _____. She's 5 feet 6 inches tall.

B **WHICH WORD?**

1. My grandson is ((six) sixty) years old.

2. She's middle-aged. She's (fifty five) years old.

3. My wife is five (inches feet) tall.

4. My brother weighs 100 (years pounds).

5. My granddaughter is young. She's three years (age old).

C **LISTENING**

Listen and circle the words you hear.

1. (5 feet 9 inches)   5 feet 4 inches

2. 150 pounds   130 pounds

3. height   weight

4. tall   old

5. height   weight

6. 5 feet 6 inches   6 feet 5 inches

7. weight   eight

8. 99 pounds   89 pounds

A MATCHING

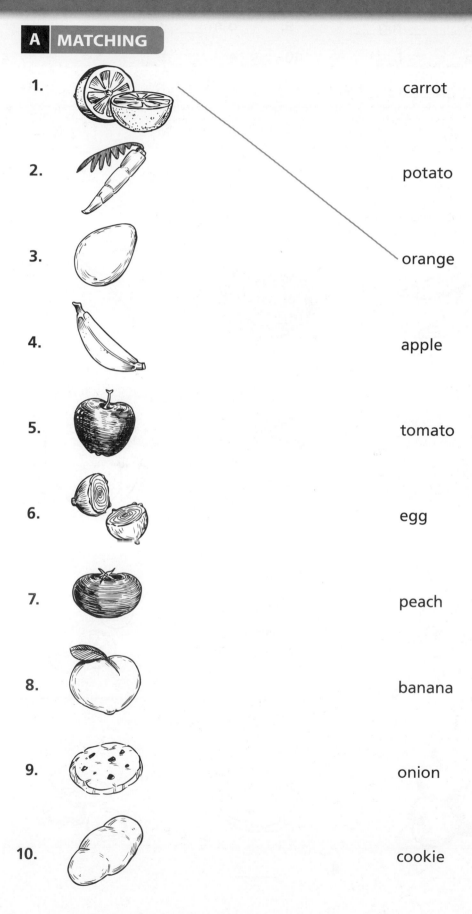

1.   carrot

2.   potato

3.   orange

4.   apple

5.   tomato

6.   egg

7.   peach

8.   banana

9.   onion

10.   cookie

1. p _o_ _t_ a t _o_

2. __ a __ a n __

3. __ n __ o n

4. __ o o k __ __ s

5. o __ __ __ n g __

6. a __ __ l __

7. __ a __ r __ t s

8. __ g __ s

9. __ o m __ __ o

10. __ e __ __ h

C LISTENING

Listen and put a check (✓) under the food you hear.

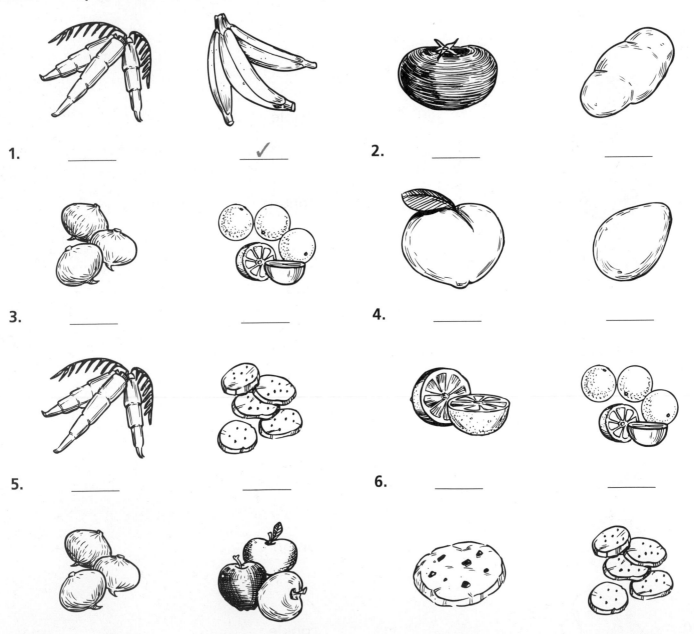

1. _____   __✓__   2. _____   _____

3. _____   _____   4. _____   _____

5. _____   _____   6. _____   _____

7. _____   _____   8. _____   _____

A MATCHING

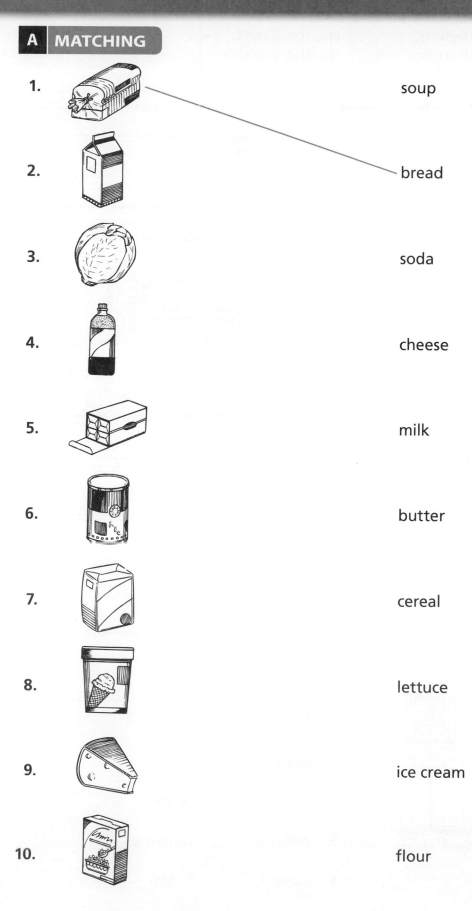

1.   soup

2.   bread

3.   soda

4.   cheese

5.   milk

6.   butter

7.   cereal

8.   lettuce

9.   ice cream

10.   flour

> Yes, there is.   No, there isn't.
> Yes, there are.   No, there aren't.

1. Is there any butter?   _Yes, there is._

2. Are there any bananas?   _No, there aren't._

3. Is there any lettuce?   _____

4. Is there any cheese?   _____

5. Are there any oranges?   _____

6. Are there any apples?   _____

7. Is there any bread?   _____

8. Are there any eggs?   _____

9. Are there any peaches?   _____

10. Is there any milk?   _____

11. Are there any onions?   _____

12. Is there any sugar?   _____

C LISTENING

Listen and circle the word you hear.

1. cheese   (milk)

2. bread   lettuce

3. soup   soda

4. ice cream   cereal

5. potatoes   tomatoes

6. sugar   butter

A WHICH WORD?

1. Milk ((is)   are) in Aisle 2.

2. Oranges (is   are) in Aisle 9.

3. Butter (is   are) in Aisle 1.

4. Bread (is   are) in Aisle 7.

5. Potatoes (is   are) in Aisle 6.

6. Cheese (is   are) in Aisle 2.

B WHICH GROUP?

| apple | banana | carrot | lettuce | onion | orange | peach | potato |

Fruits	Vegetables
apple	

C FOODS I LIKE AND FOODS I DON'T LIKE

Put a check (✓) next to the foods you like. Put an X next to the foods you don't like.

I like ice cream.

I don't like tomatoes.

	apples		cereal		lettuce		potatoes
	bananas		cheese		milk		soda
	bread		cookies		onions		soup
	butter		eggs		oranges		sugar
	carrots		ice cream		peaches		tomatoes

A MATCHING

1. a quart of   bread

2. a bottle of   sugar

3. a can of   bananas

4. a loaf of   milk

5. a pound of   cookies

6. a bunch of   soda

7. a box of   eggs

8. a bag of   cheese

9. a jar of   soup

10. a dozen   mayonnaise

B LISTENING

Listen and put a check (✓) under the correct shopping list.

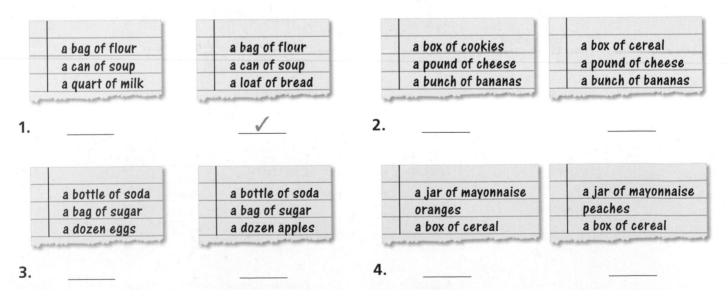

a bag of flour	a bag of flour	a box of cookies	a box of cereal
a can of soup	a can of soup	a pound of cheese	a pound of cheese
a quart of milk	a loaf of bread	a bunch of bananas	a bunch of bananas

1. _____   ✓   2. _____   _____

a bottle of soda	a bottle of soda	a jar of mayonnaise	a jar of mayonnaise
a bag of sugar	a bag of sugar	oranges	peaches
a dozen eggs	a dozen apples	a box of cereal	a box of cereal

3. _____   _____   4. _____   _____

C | WORD SEARCH

a ____ of soup   a ____ of cheese   a ____ of soda   a ____ of sugar

a ____ of bread   a ____ of cookies   a ____ of mayonnaise   a ____ eggs

a ____ of bananas   a ____ of milk

```
H   L   R   P   M   N   R   Y   S   T   P   R   J
J   C   A   N   T   M   U   A   N   S   O   A   A
I   A   N   Q   R   Y   L   O   A   F   U   E   G
R   L   O   F   F   I   S   R   A   R   N   G   G
N   P   T   A   I   B   U   B   R   D   B   R   N
P   O   U   N   D   R   B   O   T   T   U   Y   E
O   O   T   L   L   R   S   X   B   U   N   H   C
U   W   U   B   E   R   Q   A   R   T   C   Y   D
D   M   B   O   T   T   L   E   F   B   H   S   O
N   D   I   T   S   T   Y   S   T   L   O   H   Z
J   A   R   T   N   H   B   A   X   K   B   G   E
S   T   I   E   E   D   R   B   O   T   A   R   N
L   I   N   L   Q   U   A   R   T   R   G   E   B
C   A   M   E   D   O   Z   N   E   Y   O   R   E
```

D | WHAT ARE THEY SAYING?

Complete the conversation. Practice it with another student.

A. What do we need at the supermarket?

B. We need _____

_____

_____

_____

_____

_____ .

A MATCHING

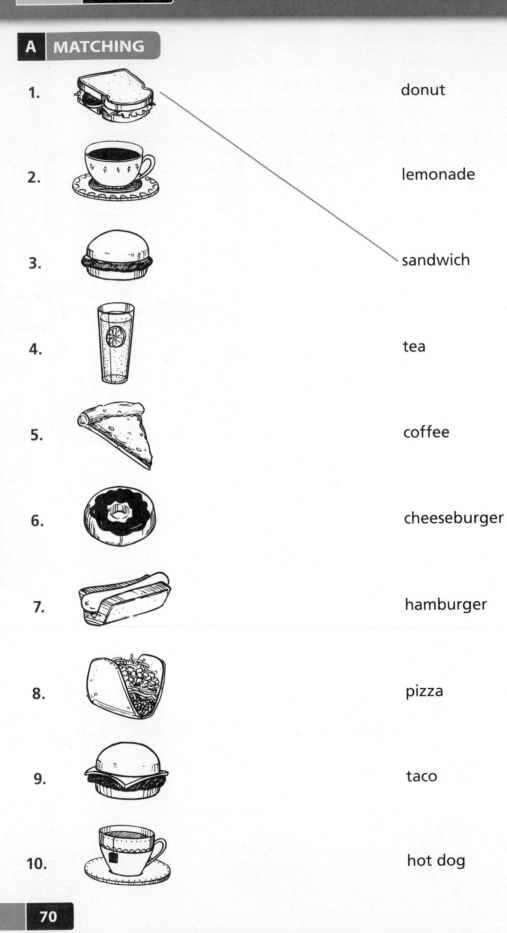

1.   donut

2.   lemonade

3.   sandwich

4.   tea

5.   coffee

6.   cheeseburger

7.   hamburger

8.   pizza

9.   taco

10.   hot dog

Listen and circle the word you hear.

1. taco   (hot dog)   4. pizza   cheeseburger
2. tea   coffee   5. taco   tea
3. sandwich hamburger   6. hamburger   lemonade

C CROSSWORD

Across

2. 3. 5.

7. 9.

Down

1. 4. 5.

6. 8.

| coffee | hot dogs | milk | sandwiches | tacos |
| donuts | lemonade | pizza | soda | tea |

Things I Eat

donuts

_____

_____

_____

_____

Things I Drink

coffee

_____

_____

_____

_____

E **WHICH WORD?**

1. I'm looking for ((milk)   orange).

2. We need a box of (bread   cereal).

3. There aren't any more (lettuce   apples).

4. I'm looking for a (egg   peach).

5. We need a jar of (sugar   mayonnaise).

6. I'd like a (sandwich   butter), please.

7. I'm looking for an (cookie   onion).

8. There isn't any more (sugar   banana).

9. We need a (quart of   dozen of) milk.

10. I'd like (taco   tea), please.

A MATCHING

1. Please get a pound of cheese.   1/2 doz.

2. Please get a dozen eggs.   1 qt.

3. Please get a quart of orange juice.   3 qts.

4. Please get half a dozen eggs.   1/2 lb.

5. Please get half a pound of cheese.   1 lb.

6. Please get two pounds of apples.   1 doz.

7. Please get three quarts of milk.   2 lbs.

B WHICH WORD?

1. Please get a pound of ((butter)   soup) at the supermarket.

2. Please get a quart of (carrots   milk) at the supermarket.

3. We need two dozen (eggs   butter) at the supermarket.

4. We need half a pound of (lettuce   potatoes) at the supermarket.

5. Please get two quarts of (cookies   ice cream) at the supermarket.

6. Please get half a dozen (peaches   sugar) at the supermarket.

7. We need two or three pounds of (bread   apples) at the supermarket.

C LISTENING

Listen and put a check (✓) under the correct amount.

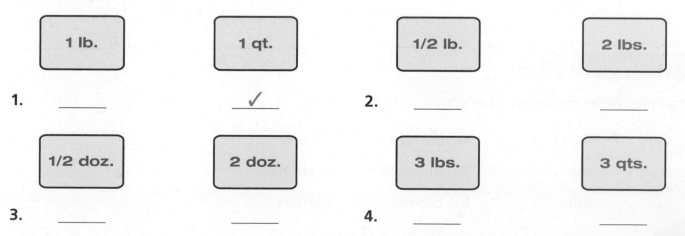

| 1 lb. | 1 qt. | 1/2 lb. | 2 lbs. |

1. _____   ___✓___   2. _____   _____

| 1/2 doz. | 2 doz. | 3 lbs. | 3 qts. |

3. _____   _____   4. _____   _____

A WHAT'S THE WORD?

belt	blouse	jacket	shirt	sweater	umbrella
coat	dress	necklace	suit	tie	watch

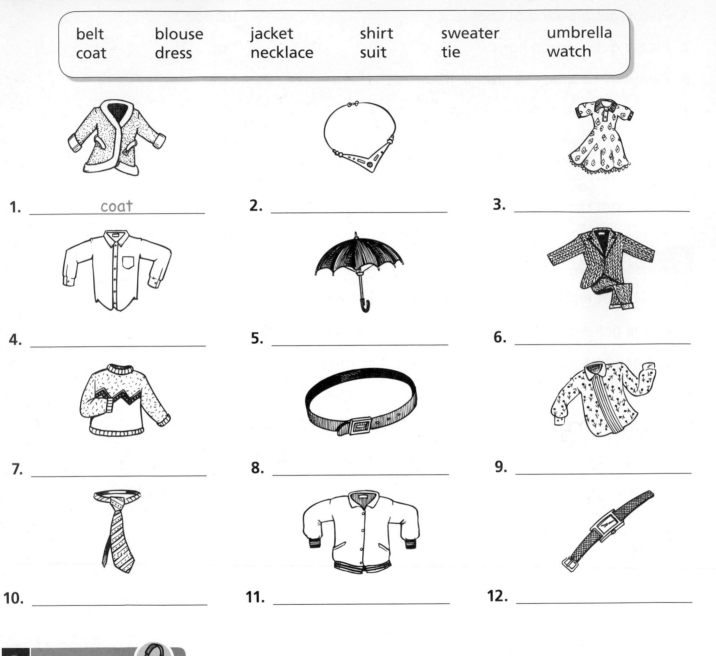

1. _coat_

2. _____

3. _____

4. _____

5. _____

6. _____

7. _____

8. _____

9. _____

10. _____

11. _____

12. _____

B LISTENING

Listen and circle the word you hear.

1. (shirt)   shirts

2. coat   coats

3. suit   suits

4. blouse   blouses

5. umbrella   umbrellas

6. blouse   blouses

belt   blouse   coat   jacket   necklace   sweater   suit   umbrella

1. A. I'm looking for a _____coat_____.
   B. _____Coats_____ are over there.
   A. Thank you.

2. A. I'm looking for a _____.
   B. _____ are over there.
   A. Thank you.

3. A. I'm looking for a _____.
   B. _____ are over there.
   A. Thank you.

4. A. I'm looking for a _____.
   B. _____ are over there.
   A. Thank you.

5. A. I'm looking for a _____.
   B. _____ are over there.
   A. Thank you.

6. A. I'm looking for a _____.
   B. _____ are over there.
   A. Thank you.

7. A. I'm looking for an _____.
   B. _____ are over there.
   A. Thank you.

8. A. I'm looking for a _____.
   B. _____ are over there.
   A. Thank you.

A WHAT'S THE WORD?

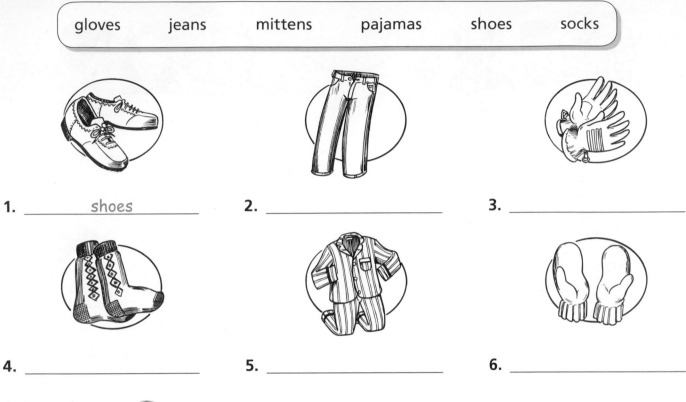

| gloves | jeans | mittens | pajamas | shoes | socks |

1. _____shoes_____   2. _____   3. _____

4. _____   5. _____   6. _____

B LISTENING 🎧

Listen and put a check (✓) under the correct picture.

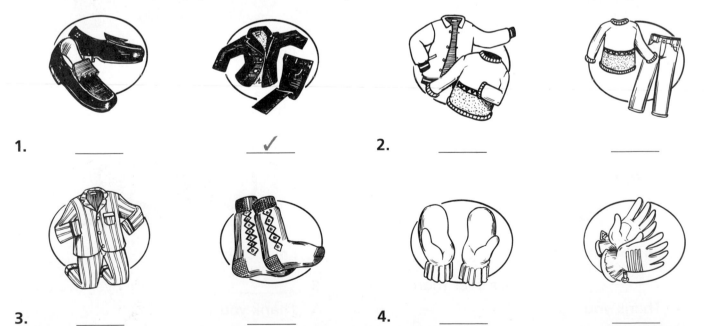

1. _____   ✓   2. _____   _____

3. _____   _____   4. _____   _____

___c___ **1.** She's wearing a coat.	_____ **4.** He's wearing gloves.
_____ **2.** He's wearing a shirt.	_____ **5.** He's wearing jeans.
_____ **3.** She's wearing a dress.	_____ **6.** She's wearing a skirt.

_____ **7.** He's wearing mittens.	_____ **10.** She's wearing a suit.
_____ **8.** She's wearing a blouse.	_____ **11.** She's wearing a jacket.
_____ **9.** He's wearing pajamas.	_____ **12.** He's wearing a sweater.

blouse   coat   jeans   pajamas   pants   shirt   shoes   skirt   suit   watch

```
I   B   B   N   A   D   S   E   F   M   O   K   C
H   B   L   O   U   S   E   P   C   O   A   R   A
H   W   N   P   T   M   J   A   N   S   D   J   O
J   E   E   N   S   C   K   T   S   C   O   A   T
I   S   C   R   P   K   B   N   O   O   S   J   J
J   H   J   E   A   N   S   S   C   D   E   Z   S
I   I   O   M   N   R   E   Y   P   A   N   T   S
C   R   L   S   S   T   S   H   A   O   E   R   S
D   T   I   K   T   R   O   M   J   T   E   S   I
C   S   S   I   I   T   S   M   A   M   Y   K   U
T   D   E   R   R   L   S   S   M   A   R   I   T
S   H   O   E   S   J   U   E   A   S   A   R   E
S   G   R   T   J   N   I   S   S   E   Y   T   A
W   A   T   C   H   N   T   S   O   W   K   D   P
```

E WHICH ONE DOESN'T BELONG?

1. jeans   shirt   pants

2. socks   gloves   mittens

3. blouse   dress   tie

4. watch   skirt   necklace

5. shirt   sweater   socks

6. socks   coat   shoes

F WHAT ARE THEY WEARING?

Write about two students in your class. What are they wearing?

_____ is wearing _____.

_____ is wearing _____.

A MISSING LETTERS

1. g r _e_ e _n_
2. _ _ _ _ d
3. _ _ e _ _ _ _ o w
4. o _ _ a n _ _ e
5. p _ _ r _ _ _ _ e
6. _ _ l u _ _
7. _ _ l _ _ c k
8. w h _ _ _ _ e
9. _ _ _ _ n k
10. b r o _ _ _ _
11. g _ _ a _ _

B WHAT'S THE COLOR?

| brown | green | orange | red | white | yellow |

1. Tomatoes are _____red_____.
2. Lettuce is _____.
3. Bananas are _____.
4. Carrots are _____.
5. Milk is _____.
6. Coffee is _____.

Write two more sentences about colors.

7. _____

8. _____

C LISTENING

Listen and circle the word you hear.

1. (yellow)   red
2. gray   green
3. pink   purple
4. black   brown
5. gray   red
6. purple   orange

D TELL ABOUT COLORS

1. My favorite color is _____.
2. My English textbook is _____.
3. My classroom is _____.
4. My _____ is _____.

A WHICH GROUP?

blue	dress	green	medium	pants	small
brown	extra-large	jacket	mittens	red	size 10
coat	gloves	large	orange	size 34	yellow

Clothing	Size	Color
coat		

B LISTENING

Listen and circle the word you hear.

1. (large)   extra-large   **3.** 11   7   **5.** 9   5

2. black   brown   **4.** long   large   **6.** small   tall

C MATCHING

1. Sweaters are   black jacket.

2. I'm looking for a   12.

3. This shirt   gray socks.

4. I'm looking for size   over there.

5. These pants   is too big.

6. I'm looking for a pair of   are too tight.

A WHAT'S THE PRICE?

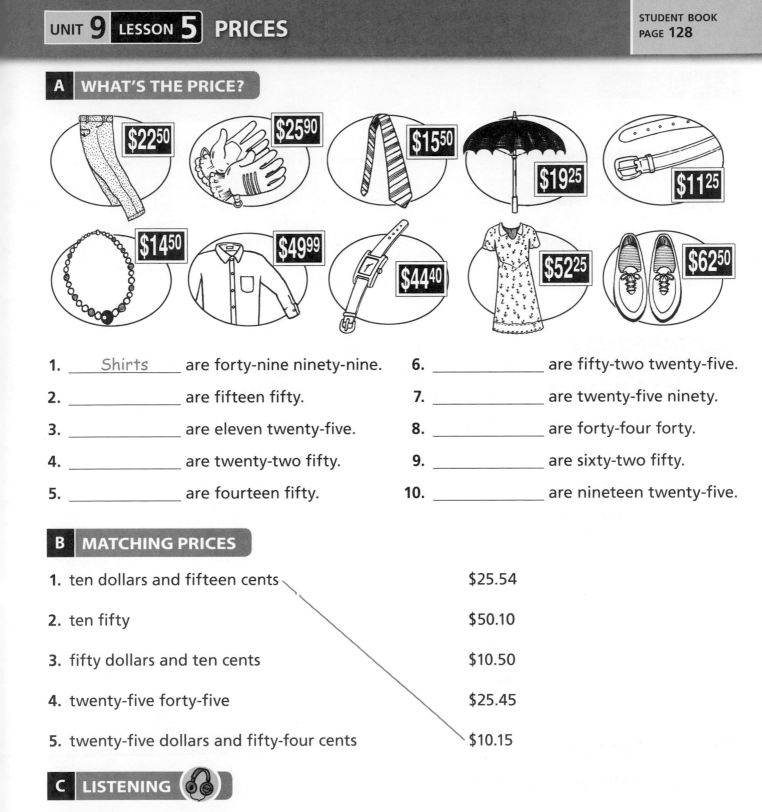

1. ___Shirts___ are forty-nine ninety-nine.

2. _____ are fifteen fifty.

3. _____ are eleven twenty-five.

4. _____ are twenty-two fifty.

5. _____ are fourteen fifty.

6. _____ are fifty-two twenty-five.

7. _____ are twenty-five ninety.

8. _____ are forty-four forty.

9. _____ are sixty-two fifty.

10. _____ are nineteen twenty-five.

B MATCHING PRICES

1. ten dollars and fifteen cents $25.54

2. ten fifty $50.10

3. fifty dollars and ten cents $10.50

4. twenty-five forty-five $25.45

5. twenty-five dollars and fifty-four cents $10.15

C LISTENING

Listen and circle the price you hear.

1. $49.00   ($45.00)   4. $15.50 $19.50   7. $8.70 $18.77

2. $36.00 $46.00   5. $16.00 $60.00   8. $69.50 $96.50

3. $51.00 $61.00   6. $19.99 $9.99   9. $32.65 $23.55

A   MATCHING

1. What's his age?

2. What's his height?

3. What's his marital status?

4. What size are you looking for?

5. What's the price of the shirt?

He's divorced.

Large.

He's old.

Twenty-five dollars.

He's short.

B   WHICH WORD?

1. I'm from (Vietnamese   Vietnam).

2. He isn't tall, and he isn't short. He's average (height   weight).

3. My sister has (blue   blond) eyes.

4. I speak (Morocco   Arabic).

5. I'm looking for a (banana   carrots).

6. We need a (can   bag) of soup.

7. I'm looking for a pair of (socks   dress).

8. There aren't any more (milk   eggs).

9. This shirt is too (small   medium).

10. We need a loaf of (bananas   bread).

C   LISTENING

Listen and circle the words you hear.

1. hungry   angry

2. blouse   blouses

3. blue suit   suit blue

4. Korea   Korean

5. long   small

A MATCHING

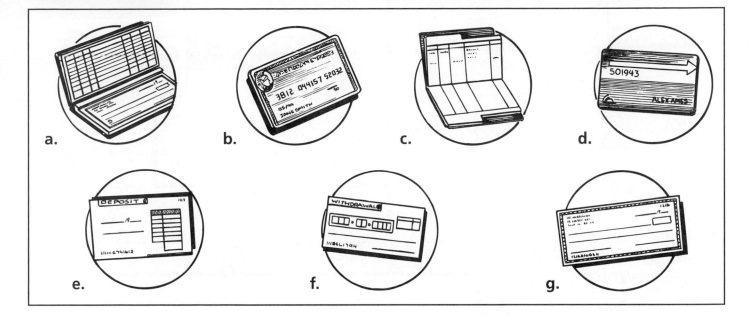

a.   b.   c.   d.

e.   f.   g.

___g___ **1.** Where's the check?   _____ **5.** Where's the credit card?

_____ **2.** Where's the deposit slip?   _____ **6.** Where's the bank book?

_____ **3.** Where's the withdrawal slip? _____ **7.** Where's the checkbook?

_____ **4.** Where's the ATM card?

B LISTENING

Listen and write the number next to the correct picture.

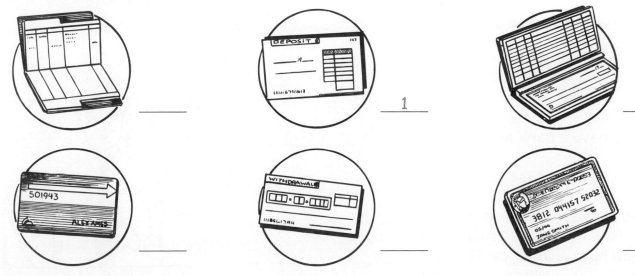

_____   __1__   _____

_____   _____   _____

C CROSSWORD

Across

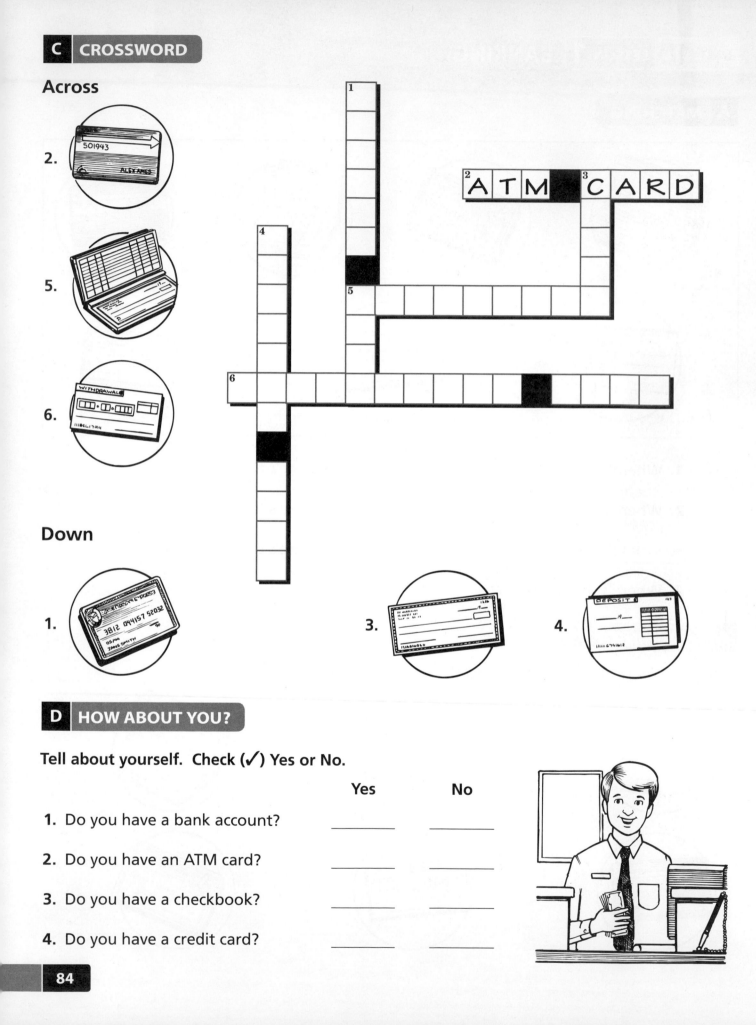

2.

5.

6.

2 ATM 3 CARD

Down

1.

3.

4.

D HOW ABOUT YOU?

Tell about yourself. Check (✓) Yes or No.

	Yes	No
1. Do you have a bank account?	_____	_____
2. Do you have an ATM card?	_____	_____
3. Do you have a checkbook?	_____	_____
4. Do you have a credit card?	_____	_____

A MATCHING

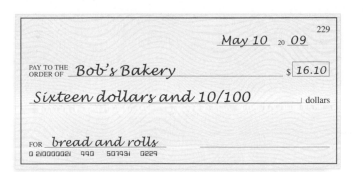

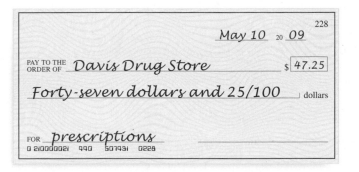

1. I'm writing a check to Davis Drug Store for   sixty-five ninety.

2. I'm writing a check to Dr. Lee for   sixteen dollars and ten cents.

3. I'm writing a check to Central Supermarket for   forty-seven twenty-five.

4. I'm writing a check to City Hospital for   ninety-five fifteen.

5. I'm writing a check to Bob's Bakery for   seventy-five dollars.

6. I'm writing a check to Gray's Department Store for   one hundred fifty dollars.

Write today's date, the dollar amounts in numbers and words, and sign your name.

1. $250.00

2. $70.00

3. $45.15

4. $471.30

5. $83.99

233

_____ 20 ____

PAY TO THE
ORDER OF *Westville Hospital* $ [   ]

_____ dollars

FOR *blood tests*   _____
0 210000021 990 507931 0233

234

_____ 20 ____

PAY TO THE
ORDER OF *Dr. Lopez* $ [   ]

_____ dollars

FOR *office visit*   _____
0 210000021 990 507931 0234

235

_____ 20 ____

PAY TO THE
ORDER OF *Cityside Gas* $ [   ]

_____ dollars

FOR *September bill*   _____
0 210000021 990 507931 0235

236

_____ 20 ____

PAY TO THE
ORDER OF *VistaCard* $ [   ]

_____ dollars

FOR *monthly bill*   _____
0 210000021 990 507931 0236

237

_____ 20 ____

PAY TO THE
ORDER OF *Furniture World* $ [   ]

_____ dollars

FOR *chairs*   _____
0 210000021 990 507931 0237

A MATCHING

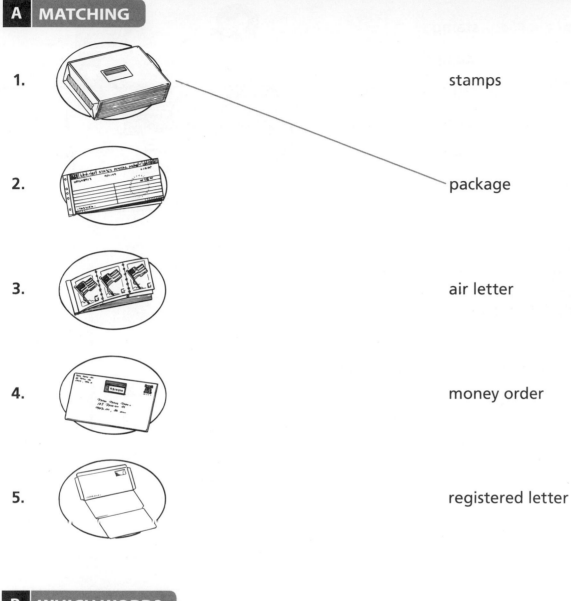

1. stamps

2. package

3. air letter

4. money order

5. registered letter

B WHICH WORD?

1. I want to buy ((stamps)   a package).

2. You can buy (a letter   an air letter)
   at the next window.

3. I want to mail (a stamp   a package).

4. You can send (stamps   a registered letter)
   at the next window.

5. You can (mail   buy) that package
   at window number 1.

Listen and circle the word you hear.

1. (package)   stamp

2. stamp   stamps

3. money order   registered letter

4. air letter   letter

5. close   open

6. 7   next

D AN ENVELOPE

Elena Montero
1200 Lake Avenue
Miami, FL 74354

Elizabeth Chen
4975 Maple Street
Chicago, IL 60604

1. Who is this letter going to?   _____

2. What's the return address?   _____

_____

Address this envelope to a friend, a family member, or another student in your class.

A HOW MUCH MONEY?

1. A. That's $45.50.

B. Here's <u>$50.00</u>.

A. Your change is <u>$4.50</u>.

2. A. That's $16.00.

B. Here's _____.

A. Your change is _____.

3. A. That's $63.50.

B. Here's _____.

A. Your change is _____.

4. A. That's $32.55.

B. Here's _____.

A. Your change is _____.

5. A. That's $26.80.

B. Here's _____.

A. Your change is _____.

6. A. That's $71.25.

B. Here's _____.

A. Your change is _____.

7. A. That's $13.10.

B. Here's _____.

A. Your change is _____.

8. A. That's $94.40.

B. Here's _____.

A. Your change is _____.

9. A. That's $12.95.

B. Here's _____.

A. Your change is _____.

B LISTENING

Listen and circle the correct amount.

1. ($9.50) $5.50   **3.** $6.19 $6.90   **5.** $7.50 $7.15

2. $3.40 $3.14   **4.** $.30 $30.00   **6.** $1.80 $11.80

A WHAT'S THE WORD?

| backache | cough | fever | sore throat | toothache |
| cold | earache | headache | stomachache | |

1. ____headache____

2. _____

3. _____

4. _____

5. _____

6. _____

7. _____

8. _____

9. _____

B LISTENING

Listen and write the number under the correct picture.

_____   _____   _____   __1__   _____

1. I (**have** has) a cough.
2. She (have has) a toothache.
3. You (have has) a stomachache.
4. He (have has) a backache.

5. You (have has) a sore throat.
6. My wife (have has) a cold.
7. My husband (have has) a headache, and I (have has) an earache.

D LISTENING

Listen and circle the word you hear.

1. **neck** nose
2. finger foot
3. head leg

4. ear eye
5. back hand
6. eye arm

E WORD SEARCH

cold	stomachache	earache	sore throat	cough
fever	toothache	headache	backache	

```
L  A  C  H  H  E  A  D  T  H  R  O  T  E
S  H  L  T  O  O  T  R  Y  S  T  P  R  H
T  C  O  L  D  T  A  H  E  D  A  C  H  E
O  E  A  N  Q  S  R  F  E  V  E  R  A  S
C  A  U  G  H  L  I  S  R  A  R  N  G  T
A  C  P  S  T  E  M  A  H  C  R  E  R  O
T  O  O  T  H  A  C  H  E  T  T  E  Y  M
Y  U  H  Y  E  R  A  A  O  T  H  N  R  A
C  G  E  U  B  A  C  A  C  H  E  T  Y  C
O  H  A  S  O  C  H  H  A  C  K  S  S  H
U  T  D  I  T  H  T  Y  S  T  L  O  A  A
G  D  A  Y  H  E  A  D  A  C  H  E  O  C
S  O  R  E  T  H  R  O  A  T  D  H  R  H
C  L  I  N  E  Y  N  A  Y  P  R  E  E  E
Z  E  R  A  C  H  B  A  C  K  A  C  H  E
```

A MATCHING

 1.

2.

 3.

4.

5.

 6.

You should use cold medicine.

You should use aspirin.

You should use ear drops.

You should use cough syrup.

You should use antacid tablets.

You should use throat lozenges.

B LISTENING

Listen and write the number under the correct picture.

_____ ___1___ _____ _____ _____ _____

C CROSSWORD

antacid tablets   aspirin   cold medicine   cough syrup   ear drops   throat lozenges

Across

2.

5.

6.

Down

1.

3.

4.

D WHICH ONE DOESN'T BELONG?

1. earache	toothache	(throat lozenges)	sore throat
2. cold	ear drops	aspirin	cold medicine
3. stomachache	cough syrup	headache	cough
4. earache	toothache	fever	stomachache
5. backache	cough	medicine	cold

| antacid tablets | aspirin | cold medicine | cough syrup | ear drops | throat lozenges |

1   2   3   4   5   6

COUGH MED

COLD

1. Where can I find _____cold medicine_____?   Look in Aisle 4.

2. Where can I find _____?   Look in Aisle 6.

3. Where can I find _____?   Look in Aisle 2.

4. Where can I find _____?   Look in Aisle 3.

5. Where can I find _____?   Look in Aisle 1.

6. Where can I find _____?   Look in Aisle 5.

F | **MATCHING**

1. cold   lozenges

2. throat   syrup

3. antacid   medicine

4. cough   tablets

G | **LISTENING** 🎧

Listen and circle the words you hear.

1. (antacid tablets)   aspirin   4. earache   ear drops

2. cough   cough syrup   5. Aisle 11   Aisle 7

3. Aisle 9   Aisle 5   6. throat lozenges   sore throat

A WHAT'S THE WORD?

A.
Doctor's 1
Drug Store
office.

B.
Excuse 2
Hello
. This is Gloria Mendoza. I want to make an
ailment 3
appointment
.

A. What's the
medicine 4
problem
?

B. I have a bad
headache 5
cough syrup
.

A. Can you come in
2:00 6
today
at
2:00 7
today
?

B. Yes. That's fine.

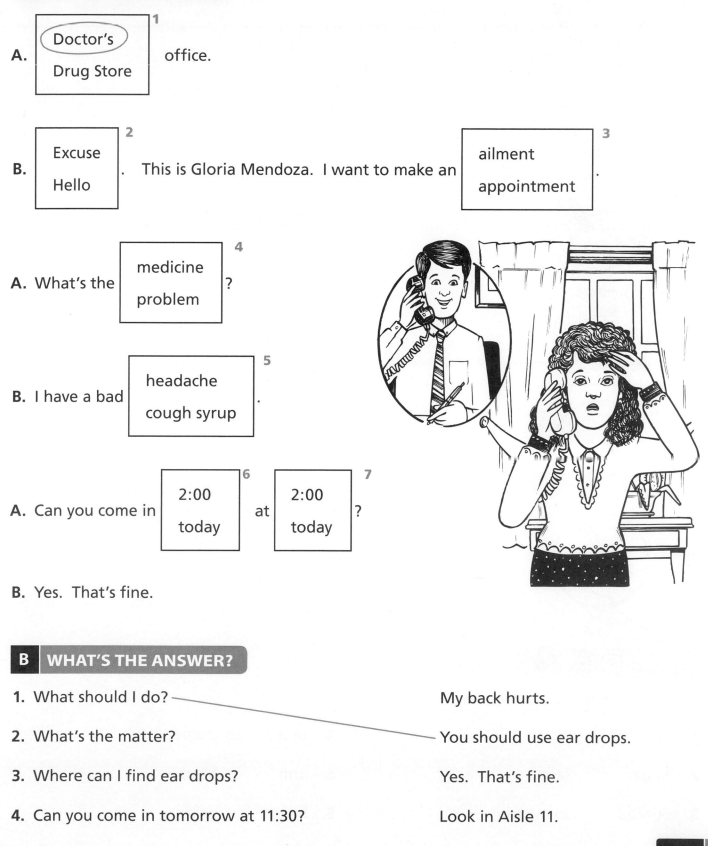

B WHAT'S THE ANSWER?

1. What should I do?   My back hurts.

2. What's the matter?   You should use ear drops.

3. Where can I find ear drops?   Yes. That's fine.

4. Can you come in tomorrow at 11:30?   Look in Aisle 11.

95

1.    I broke my leg.

2.    I burned my hand.

3.    I cut my face.

4.   I cut my finger.

5.   I sprained my wrist.

6.    I broke my arm.

D LISTENING

Listen and circle the word you hear.

1. (arm)   leg   4. broke   burned

2. finger   face   5. arm   hand

3. burned   sprained   6. hear   ear

A MATCHING

1. You should exercise   one vitamin every day.

2. You should eat   six glasses of water a day.

3. You should drink   thirty minutes every day.

4. You should take   eight hours every day.

5. You should sleep   three healthy meals a day.

B HOW ABOUT YOU?

Circle the correct word in each question, and then check (✓) Yes or No.

	Yes	No
1. Do you (drink (exercise)) a half hour every day?	_____	_____
2. Do you (eat drink) 5 or 6 glasses of water every day?	_____	_____
3. Do you (sleep eat) 8 hours every night?	_____	_____
4. Do you (drink take) a vitamin every day?	_____	_____
5. Do you (take eat) 3 healthy meals every day?	_____	_____

C WHAT'S THE WORD?

> address   ambulance   head   hurt   number   Operator

A. Emergency ____Operator____ [1].

B. My husband just fell and _____ [2] his _____ [3] very badly. He can't move.

Please send an _____ [4] right away.

A. What's your _____ [5]?

B. 1520 Tyler Avenue in Westville.

A. And your telephone _____ [6]?

B. 555–2978.

A CROSSWORD

| aisle | capsule | medicine | pill | tablet | teaspoon |

Across

2. Take one _____ before each meal.

5. Take one _____ once a day.

6. Take one _____ four times a day.

Down

1. Here's your _____.

3. Look in _____ 7 for ear drops.

4. Take one _____ twice a day.

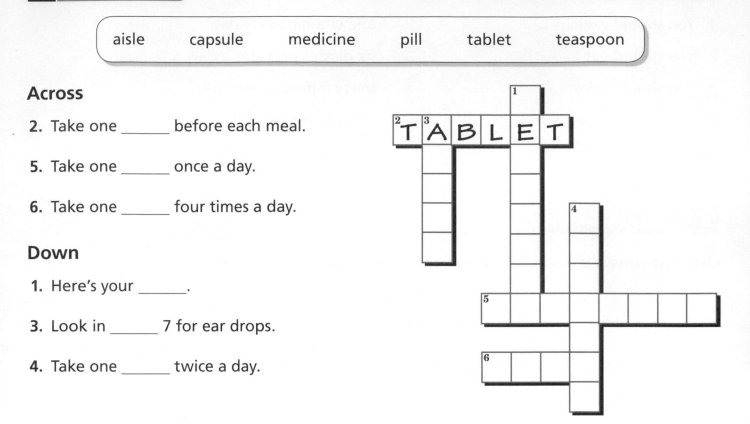

B LISTENING

Listen and choose the correct answer.

1. a. 1 tablet 2X/day   b. 2 tablets 1X/day

2. a. 3 pills 2X/day   b. 2 pills 3X/day

3. a. 3 caps 3X/day   b. 2 caps 3X/day

4. a. 2 tsps. before meals   b. 2 tsps. after meals

5. a. 1 cap. before meals   b. 1 cap. after meals

6. a. 4 tablets 2X/day   b. 4 caps. 2X/day

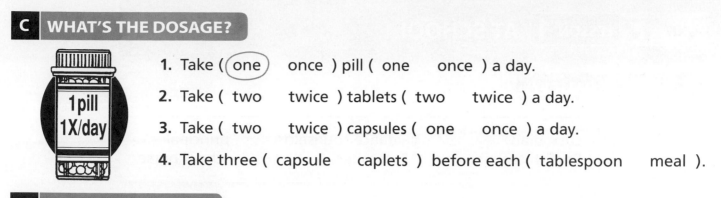

1. Take (one   once) pill (one   once) a day.

2. Take (two   twice) tablets (two   twice) a day.

3. Take (two   twice) capsules (one   once) a day.

4. Take three (capsule   caplets) before each (tablespoon   meal).

D WHAT DO YOU DO?

What do you do when you have a medical problem? Complete these sentences about yourself.

1. When I have a headache, I _____

_____

_____.

2. When I have a cough, I _____

_____

_____.

3. When I have a backache, I _____

_____

_____.

4. When I have cold, I _____

_____

_____.

5. When I have a sore throat, I _____

_____

_____.

6. When I have a stomachache, I _____

_____

_____.

A WHO ARE THEY?

| custodian | guidance counselor | principal |
| English teacher | P.E. teacher | school nurse |

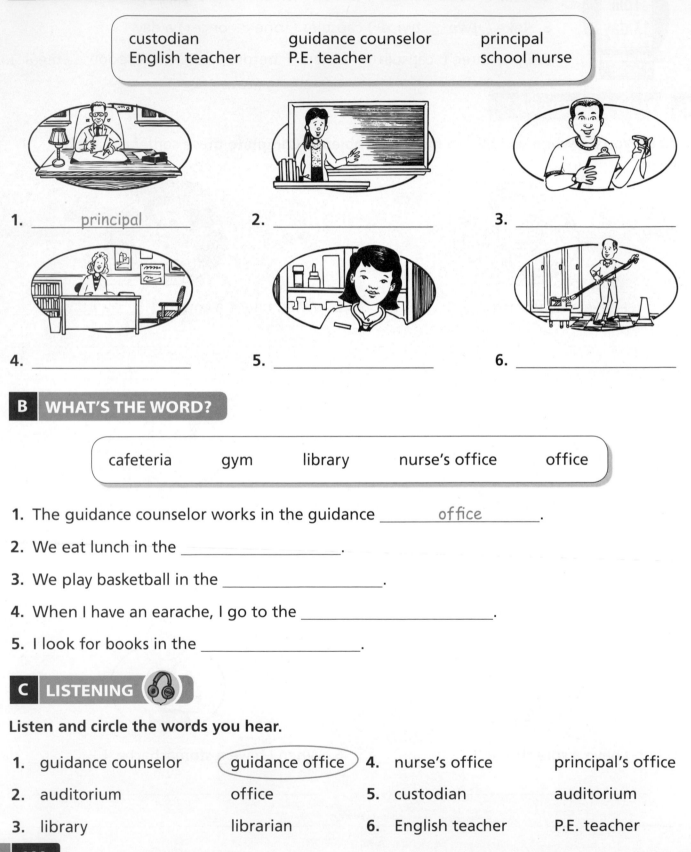

1. _____principal_____

2. _____

3. _____

4. _____

5. _____

6. _____

B WHAT'S THE WORD?

| cafeteria | gym | library | nurse's office | office |

1. The guidance counselor works in the guidance _____office_____ .

2. We eat lunch in the _____ .

3. We play basketball in the _____ .

4. When I have an earache, I go to the _____ .

5. I look for books in the _____ .

C LISTENING

Listen and circle the words you hear.

1. guidance counselor   (guidance office)   4. nurse's office   principal's office

2. auditorium   office   5. custodian   auditorium

3. library   librarian   6. English teacher   P.E. teacher

WHICH ONE DOESN'T BELONG?

1. library   cafeteria   (principal)   classroom

2. principal   English teacher   guidance counselor principal's office

3. gym   nurse's office   principal's office guidance office

4. librarian   library   custodian   school nurse

E **CROSSWORD**

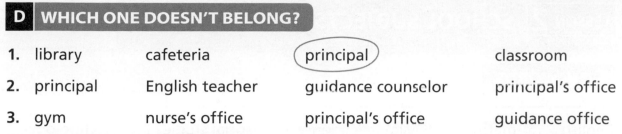

auditorium   custodian   gym   principal's office
cafeteria   guidance office   nurse's office teacher

Across

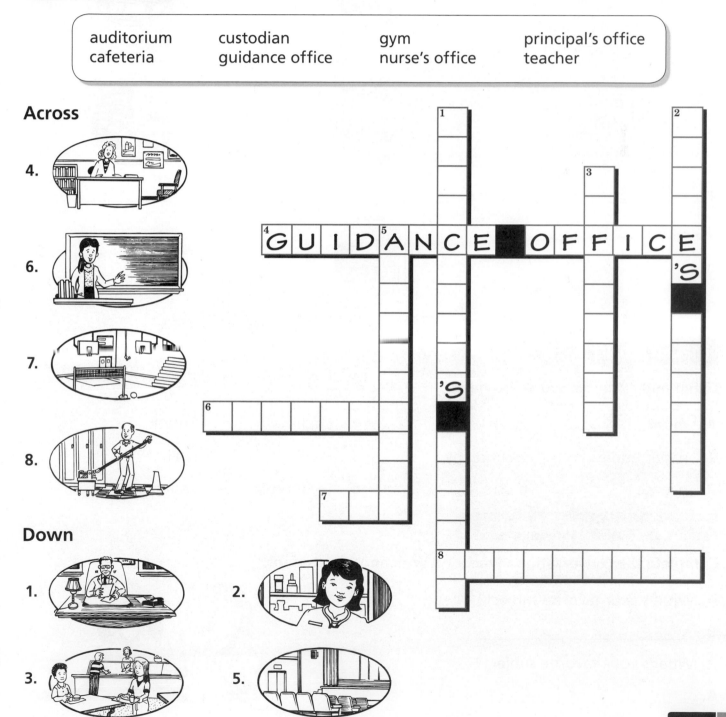

4.

6.

7.

8.

Down

1.

3.   2.   5.

A WHAT'S THE WORD?

art   English   math   music   science   social studies   technology

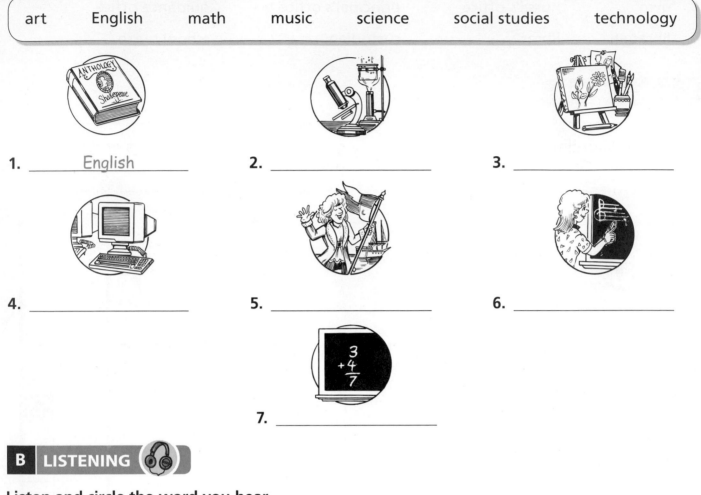

1. _____English_____

2. _____

3. _____

4. _____

5. _____

6. _____

7. _____

B LISTENING

Listen and circle the word you hear.

1. (music)   math   4. English   math

2. social studies   technology   5. math   art

3. science   music   6. technology   science

C WHAT ARE THEY SAYING?

Complete the conversation. Practice it with another student.

A. What's your favorite subject?

B. _____.

What's YOUR favorite subject?

A. _____.

A WHAT'S THE WORD?

band   basketball   choir   drama   football   orchestra

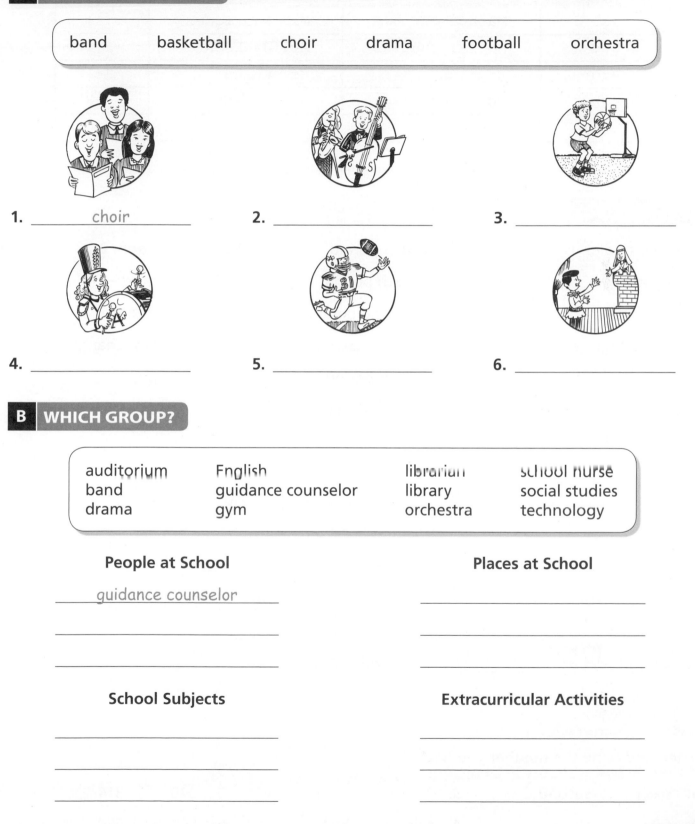

1. _____choir_____

2. _____

3. _____

4. _____

5. _____

6. _____

B WHICH GROUP?

auditorium	English	librarian	school nurse
band	guidance counselor	library	social studies
drama	gym	orchestra	technology

People at School

_____guidance counselor_____

_____

_____

Places at School

_____

_____

School Subjects

_____

_____

_____

Extracurricular Activities

_____

_____

_____

Period	Class	Teacher	Room
1st	Math	Ms. Rodriguez	134
2nd	Social Studies	Mr. Jackson	211
3rd	English	Ms. Chang	341
4th	Science	Mr. Miller	128
5th	Music	Miss Yamamoto	14
6th	Art	Mr. Williams	217

A   MATCHING

1. social studies	first period	Room 211
2. English	sixth period	music
3. Mr. Miller	second period	Room 134
4. Ms. Rodriguez	fourth period	Ms. Chang
5. Room 217	fifth period	art
6. Miss Yamamoto	third period	science

B   MY CLASS SCHEDULE

1. I have science class _____fourth_____ period in Room _____one twenty-eight_____.

2. My music class is _____ period in Room _____.

3. I have art class _____ period in Room _____.

4. My social studies class is _____ period in Room _____.

5. I have math class _____ period in Room _____.

6. My English class is _____ period in Room _____.

C   LISTENING

Listen and circle the number you hear.

1.	sixth	(second)	3. fifth	sixth	5. 340	314
2.	first	third	4. third	first	6. 509	590

A MATCHING

1. Take one pill   8 hours every day.

2. Come in tomorrow at   Aisle 3.

3. You should sleep   Room 219.

4. My English class is in   3 times a day.

5. Cough syrup is in   9:30.

B WHICH WORD?

1. When I put money in the bank, I use a (withdrawal   deposit) slip.

2. I'm writing a (check   checkbook) to Tyler's Department Store.

3. You can (buy   mail) packages at the next window.

4. My wife has a sore (fever   throat).

5. When I have a stomachache, I use (throat lozenges   antacid tablets).

6. The (custodian   principal) is cleaning the auditorium.

7. My favorite subject is (social studies   soccer).

8. I cut my (toothache   finger).

9. You should (drink   exercise) thirty minutes a day.

C LISTENING

Listen and circle the word you hear.

1. $7.30 $11.30   4. library   librarian

2. back   neck   5. guidance   science

3. burned   sprained   6. drama   soccer

A WHAT'S THE OCCUPATION?

cashier   cook   delivery person   gardener   repairperson
construction worker   custodian   electrician   police officer   security guard

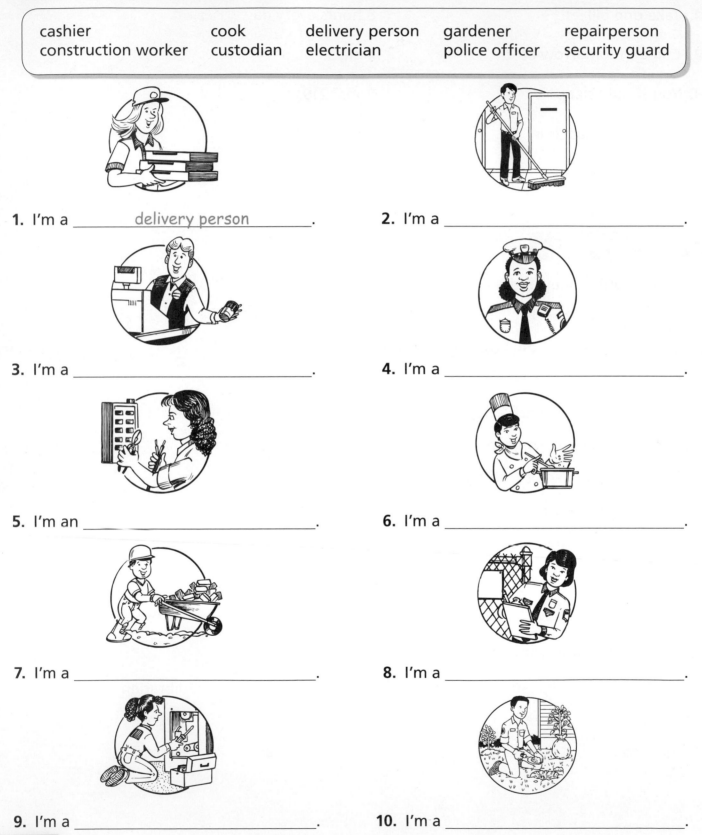

1. I'm a _____delivery person_____.

2. I'm a _____.

3. I'm a _____.

4. I'm a _____.

5. I'm an _____.

6. I'm a _____.

7. I'm a _____.

8. I'm a _____.

9. I'm a _____.

10. I'm a _____.

B LISTENING 🎧

Listen and put a check (✓) under the correct picture.

1. _____   _____ ✓   **2.** _____   _____

3. _____   _____   **4.** _____   _____

5. _____   _____   **6.** _____   _____

C MATCHING

1. delivery   guard

2. construction   person

3. security   officer

4. police   worker

D WHAT ARE THEY SAYING?

Complete the conversation. Practice it with another student.

A. What do you do?

B. I'm _____.
How about you? What do YOU do?

A. I'm _____.

A MATCHING

1. A carpenter   drives a bus.

2. A painter   drives a truck.

3. A mechanic   bakes.

4. A truck driver   repairs buildings.

5. A secretary   fixes cars.

6. A baker   fixes sinks.

7. A bus driver   paints.

8. A teacher   drives a taxi.

9. A plumber   teaches.

10. A taxi driver   types.

B LISTENING

Listen and write the number under the correct picture.

_____   1   _____   _____

_____   _____   _____   _____

A WHERE DO THEY WORK?

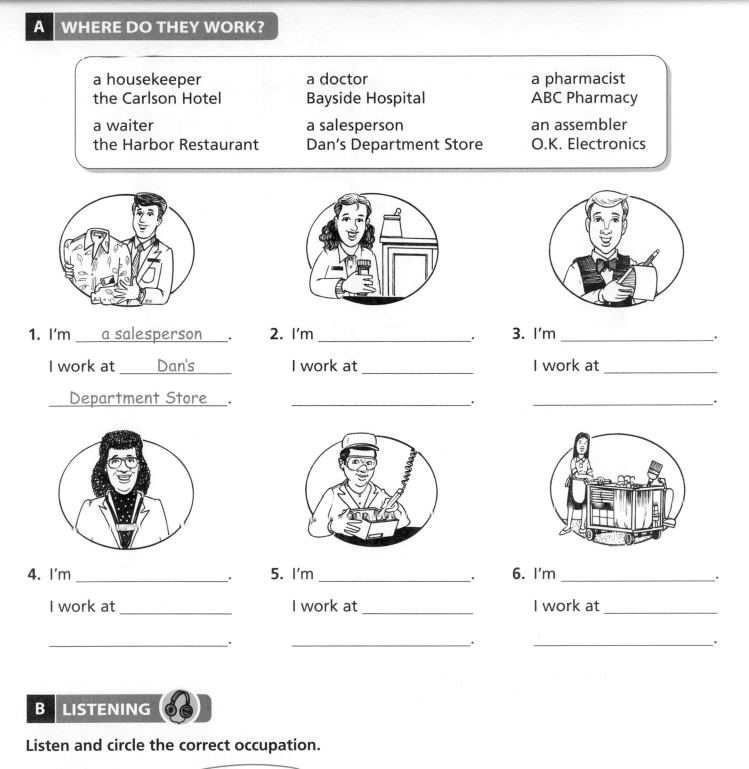

a housekeeper
the Carlson Hotel

a doctor
Bayside Hospital

a pharmacist
ABC Pharmacy

a waiter
the Harbor Restaurant

a salesperson
Dan's Department Store

an assembler
O.K. Electronics

1. I'm ____a salesperson____.

I work at ____Dan's____

____Department Store____.

2. I'm _____.

I work at _____

_____.

3. I'm _____.

I work at _____

_____.

4. I'm _____.

I work at _____

_____.

5. I'm _____.

I work at _____

_____.

6. I'm _____.

I work at _____

_____.

B LISTENING

Listen and circle the correct occupation.

1. assembler (housekeeper)

2. doctor   salesperson

3. housekeeper   waiter

4. assembler   pharmacist

5. doctor   waiter

6. salesperson   pharmacist

Across

2. I work at a restaurant. I'm a _____.

5. I work at a hotel. I'm a _____.

6. I work at a hospital. I'm a _____.

7. I work at an electronics factory.
I'm an _____.

Down

1. I work at a restaurant. I'm a _____.

3. I work at a department store. I'm a _____.

4. I work at a pharmacy. I'm a _____.

1. pharmacy   pharmacist   hospital   hotel

2. security guard   gardener   repairperson   restaurant

3. taxi driver   bus driver   housekeeper   truck driver

4. store   hotel   hospital   custodian

5. waitress   restaurant   waiter   cook

A | WHICH WORD?

1. Can you (assemble   operate) components?
2. Can you (repair   cut) hair?
3. Can you (operate   cook) equipment?
4. Can you (cut   repair) watches?
5. Can you (assemble   use) a cash register?
6. Can you (sell   operate) clothing?

B | LISTENING

Listen and put a check (✓) under the correct picture.

1. ___✓___   _____   2. _____   _____

3. _____   _____   4. _____   _____

C | TELL ABOUT YOURSELF

What can you do?

I can _____.   I can _____.

I can _____.   I can _____.

I can _____.   I can _____.

A MATCHING

1.  The supply room is down the hall.

2.  The personnel office is down the hall.

3.  The bathroom is down the hall.

4.  The mailroom is down the hall.

5.  The vending machine is down the hall.

6. 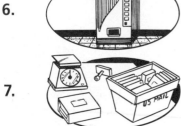 The cafeteria is down the hall.

7. The employee lounge is down the hall.

B LISTENING

Listen and circle the word you hear.

1. supply room   (mailroom)

2. cafeteria   bathroom

3. personnel office   employee lounge

4. mailroom   supply room

5. lounge   down

C WORD SEARCH

cafeteria   bathroom   employee lounge   mailroom   supply room   vending machine

```
L  A  C  H  B  A  T  R  O  O  H  C  S  F
S  U  P  L  Y  R  O  O  M  T  I  T  U  N
E  M  S  B  E  R  C  R  A  I  B  P  P  B
C  A  F  E  T  E  R  I  A  T  H  M  P  D
E  I  C  L  O  N  A  K  L  B  O  A  L  Q
V  L  U  K  O  O  T  H  C  I  H  O  Y  N
E  R  T  B  A  T  H  R  O  O  M  R  R  G
N  O  M  T  R  O  R  M  W  V  D  E  O  J
D  O  M  A  L  I  N  G  R  O  O  M  O  D
I  M  P  C  A  F  O  B  L  B  T  A  M  S
I  O  S  K  E  M  P  L  O  Y  E  E  R  H
E  M  P  L  O  Y  E  E  L  O  U  N  G  E
B  G  M  L  R  O  O  B  T  H  R  E  O  E
V  E  N  D  I  N  G  M  A  C  H  I  N  E
```

D WHAT'S THE LOCATION?

Read the sentences and write the locations on the diagram.

1. The mailroom is across from the bathroom.

2. The supply room is next to the mailroom.

3. The personnel office is across from the supply room.

4. The cafeteria is next to the personnel office.

5. The employee lounge is across from the cafeteria.

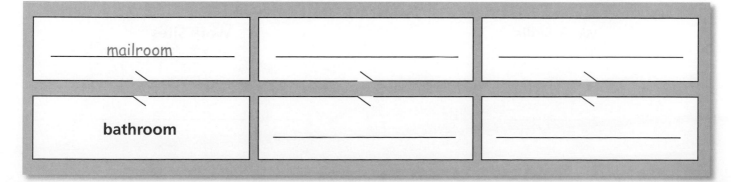

_____ mailroom _____

bathroom

A WHAT'S THE WORD?

Careful	room	safety	smoke	Thanks	wet

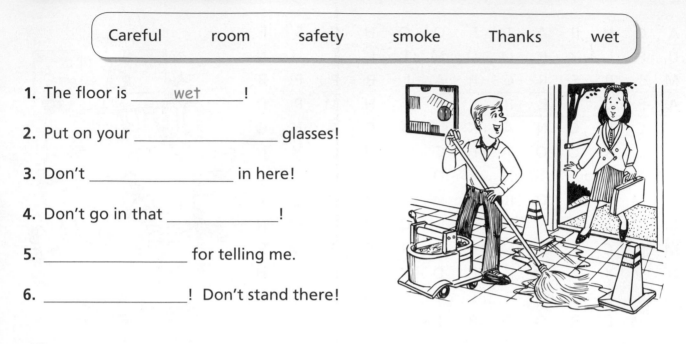

1. The floor is _____wet_____!

2. Put on your _____ glasses!

3. Don't _____ in here!

4. Don't go in that _____!

5. _____ for telling me.

6. _____! Don't stand there!

B WHICH GROUP?

Buy-Rite Pharmacy	gardener	mailroom	repair buildings
custodian	Grover Hospital	paint	security guard
drive a bus	Hi-Tech Electronics	personnel office	supply room

Occupations

custodian

_____

_____

Locations at Work

_____

_____

_____

Work Skills

_____

_____

_____

Work Sites

_____

_____

_____

A   KENJI'S WORK SCHEDULE

Day	SUN	MON	TUE	WED	THU	FRI	SAT
Start	11:00 AM	8:00 AM	8:00 AM	8:00 AM		3:00 PM	11:00 AM
End	3:00 PM	3:00 PM	3:00 PM	3:00 PM		8:00 PM	4:00 PM

1. Kenji works (five (six)) days a week.

2. He doesn't work on (Tuesday   Thursday).

3. On Sunday he works (three   four) hours.

4. On Saturday he works (four   five) hours.

5. On Monday, Tuesday, and Wednesday, he works (six   seven) hours.

6. He works in the evening on (Friday   Saturday).

7. He works a total of (thirty-three   thirty-five) hours a week.

B   PAYCHECK DEDUCTIONS

Look at Yolanda's paycheck on page 184 of the *Foundations* book. Complete the sentences.

1. Her gross pay is __$520.00__ .

2. Her state tax is _____ .

3. Her federal taxes are _____ .

4. Her health plan deduction is _____ .

5. Her social security and Medicare taxes are _____ .

6. Her total deductions are _____ .

7. After deductions, she takes home _____ .

C   LISTENING

Listen and circle the numbers you hear.

1. 5 AM to 9 PM (9 AM to 5 PM)

2. $15.00 $13.00

3. 30 hours   40 hours

4. $27.50 $25.70

5. $600.00 $700.00

6. $450.00 $415.00

A WHAT'S THE LOCATION?

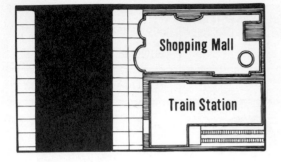

1. A. Excuse me. How do I get to the shopping mall?

B. Walk that way. The shopping mall is on the
(left (right)), (across from   next to)
the train station.

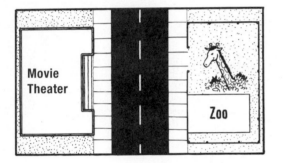

2. A. Excuse me. How do I get to the movie theater?

B. Walk that way. The movie theater is on the
(left   right), (across from   next to)
the zoo.

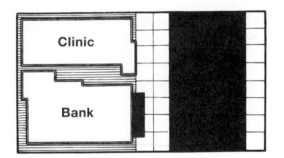

3. A. Excuse me. How do I get to the bank?

B. Walk that way. The bank is on the
(left   right), (across from   next to)
the clinic.

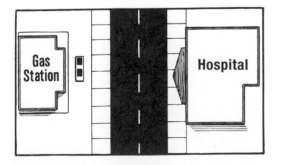

4. A. Excuse me. How do I get to the hospital?

B. Walk that way. The hospital is on the
(left   right), (across from   next to)
the gas station.

Listen and write the names on the buildings.

bakery   drug store   laundromat   library   movie theater   post office   train station

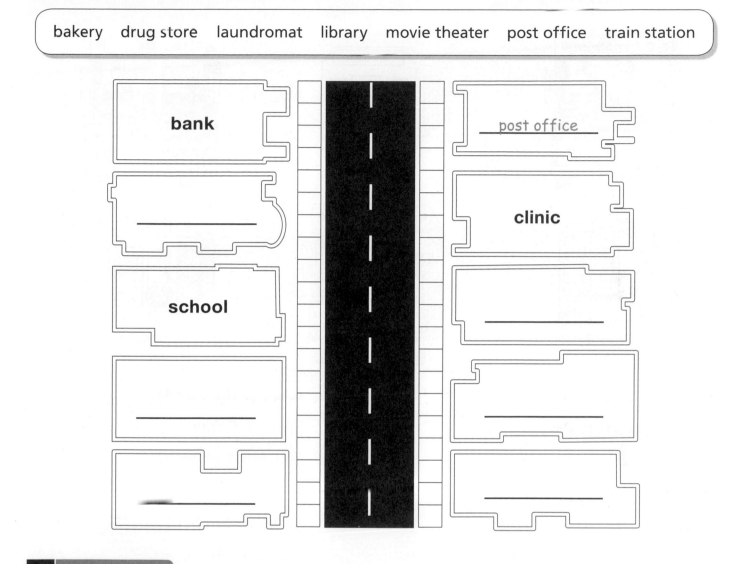

bank

post office

clinic

school

C   YES OR NO?

Look at the map in Exercise B and answer Yes or No.

1. The post office is next to the clinic.   (Yes)   No

2. The bakery is across from the school.   Yes   (No)

3. The drug store is next to the train station.   Yes   No

4. The movie theater is across from the drug store.   Yes   No

5. The library is across from the clinic.   Yes   No

6. The school is next to the movie theater.   Yes   No

7. The drug store is next to the school.   Yes   No

A WHERE DO THEY GO?

1. How do I get to the zoo?

2. How do I get to Park Street?

3. How do I get to the train station?

4. How do I get to Pine Street?

5. How do I get to the mall?

6. How do I get to River Street?

Take Bus Number 11.

Take the C Train.

Take Bus Number 12.

Take the Blue Line.

Take Bus Number 2.

Take the B Train.

B LISTENING

Listen and circle the correct answer.

1.	the E Train	⟨the D Train⟩
2.	Bus Number 5	Bus Number 9
3.	the Red Line	the Yellow Line
4.	Bus M7	Bus N11
5.	the Green Line	the D Line
6.	Bus Number 2	Bus Number 22

A MATCHING

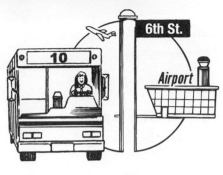

1. Where do I get off for the hospital?   Get off at Fifth Street.

2. Where do I get off for City Hall?   Get off at Central Avenue.

3. Where do I get off for the mall?   Get off at Eleventh Avenue.

4. Where do I get off for the airport?   Get off at Seventh Avenue.

5. Where do I get off for the library?   Get off at Sixth Street.

6. Where do I get off for the zoo?   Get off at Center Street.

B LISTENING

Listen and put a check (✓) under the correct street sign.

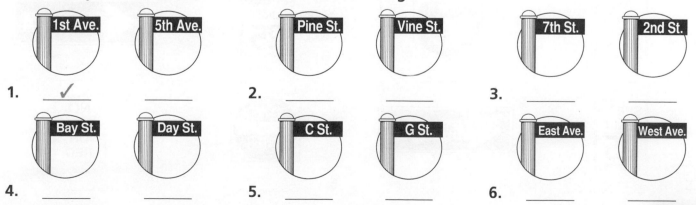

1st Ave.	5th Ave.	Pine St.	Vine St.	7th St.	2nd St.
1. ✓	___	**2.** ___ ___		**3.** ___ ___	

Bay St.	Day St.	C St.	G St.	East Ave.	West Ave.
4. ___	___	**5.** ___ ___		**6.** ___ ___	

A MATCHING

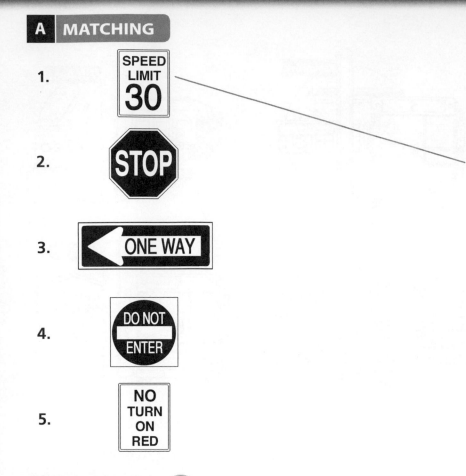

1. SPEED LIMIT 30

You can't go that way!

2. STOP

Slow down! The sign says, "Speed Limit 30."

3. ONE WAY

Don't turn yet!

4. DO NOT ENTER

You have to stop!

5. NO TURN ON RED

You can't go on that street!

B LISTENING

Listen and put a check (✓) under the correct sign.

1. SPEED LIMIT 25 _____   SPEED LIMIT 35 ✓   2. STOP _____   SPEED LIMIT 30 _____

3. NO TURN ON RED _____   DO NOT ENTER _____   4. SPEED LIMIT 25 _____   ONE WAY _____

5. SPEED LIMIT 25 _____   ONE WAY _____   6. DO NOT ENTER _____   NO TURN ON RED _____

left	people	right	school	train	U

1. No ___U___ -turn.

2. No _____ turn.

3. No _____ turn.

4. There are _____ tracks ahead.

5. Look for _____ in the street.

6. There's a _____ nearby.

D   LISTENING

Listen and circle the words you hear.

1. left   (right)

2. U-turn   school

3. people   speed limit

4. school   stop

5. that way   train tracks

A BUS NUMBER 6B

Route 6B				
Day Street	Main Street	Pine Street	Fifth Avenue	Sixth Avenue
Weekdays				
5:45 AM	6:00	6:15	6:30	6:45
6:45	7:00	7:15	7:30	7:45
7:45	8:00	8:15	8:30	8:45
8:45	9:00	9:15	9:30	9:45
10:45	11:00	11:15	11:30	11:45
12:45 PM	1:00	1:15	1:30	1:45
1:45	2:00	2:15	2:30	2:45
3:45	4:00	4:15	4:30	4:45
4:45	5:00	5:15	5:30	5:45
5:45	6:00	6:15	6:30	6:45
6:45	7:00	7:15	7:30	7:45
8:45	9:00	9:15	9:30	9:45

1. Bus Number 6B goes from ___Day Street___ to _____.

2. The first bus in the morning leaves Day Street at _____.

3. It arrives at Main Street at _____.

4. The next bus leaves Day Street at _____. It arrives at Pine Street at _____.

5. The last bus leaves Day Street at _____. It arrives at Fifth Avenue at _____.

6. It's 9:30 AM. The next bus leaves Day Street at _____.

7. It's 8:30 PM. The next bus leaves Pine Street at _____. It arrives at Sixth Avenue at _____.

B LISTENING

Listen to sentences about the schedule above. Circle the correct answers.

1. (Yes)   No
2. Yes   No
3. Yes   No
4. Yes   No
5. Yes   No

6. Yes   No
7. Yes   No
8. Yes   No
9. Yes   No
10. Yes   No

A WHAT'S THE ACTIVITY?

exercise	go jogging	go swimming	play basketball	play tennis
go dancing	go rollerblading	listen to music	play soccer	watch TV

1. I like to _____go swimming_____ .

2. I like to _____.

3. I like to _____.

4. I like to _____.

5. I like to _____.

6. I like to _____.

7. I like to _____.

8. I like to _____.

9. I like to _____.

10. I like to _____.

Across

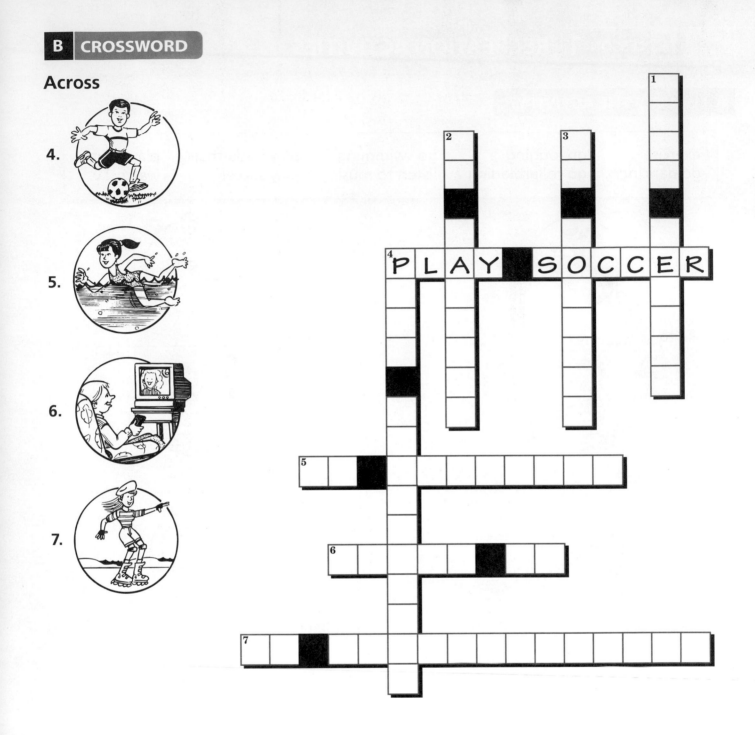

4.

5.

6.

7.

Down

1.

2.

3.

4.

Listen and write the number under the correct picture.

_____   _____   _____   1

_____   _____   _____   _____

D WHAT ARE THEY SAYING?

Complete the conversation. Practice it with another student.

A. What do you like to do in your free time?

B. I like to _____.
   How about you? What do YOU like to do?

A. _____.

E TELL ABOUT YOURSELF

Things I like to do in my free time:

_____   _____

_____   _____

_____   _____

_____   _____

A MATCHING

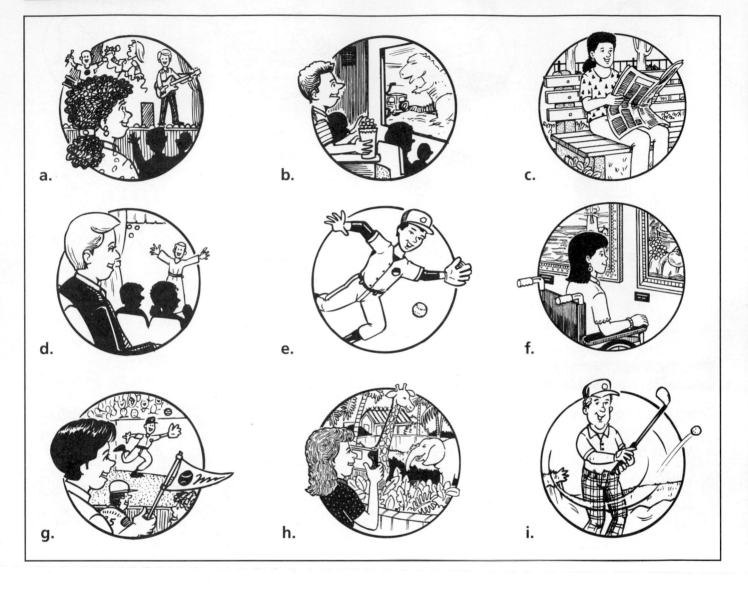

_c_ **1.** I'm going to go to the park.

_____ **2.** I'm going to see a movie.

_____ **3.** I'm going to go to a ballgame.

_____ **4.** I'm going to go to a concert.

_____ **5.** I'm going to see a play.

_____ **6.** I'm going to go to a museum.

_____ **7.** I'm going to go to the zoo.

_____ **8.** I'm going to play baseball.

_____ **9.** I'm going to play golf.

B LISTENING

Listen and put a check (✓) under the correct picture.

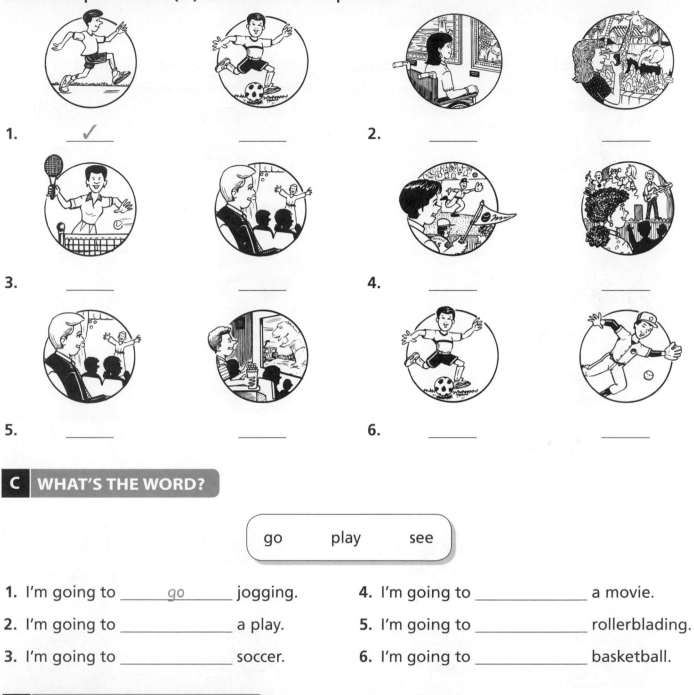

1. ____✓____   _____   2. _____   _____

3. _____   _____   4. _____   _____

5. _____   _____   6. _____   _____

C WHAT'S THE WORD?

> go   play   see

1. I'm going to ____go____ jogging.

2. I'm going to _____ a play.

3. I'm going to _____ soccer.

4. I'm going to _____ a movie.

5. I'm going to _____ rollerblading.

6. I'm going to _____ basketball.

D WHAT ARE THEY SAYING?

Complete the conversation. Practice it with another student.

A. What are you going to do tomorrow?

B. I'm going to _____.
How about you?

A. _____.

127

A WHAT DID YOU DO YESTERDAY?

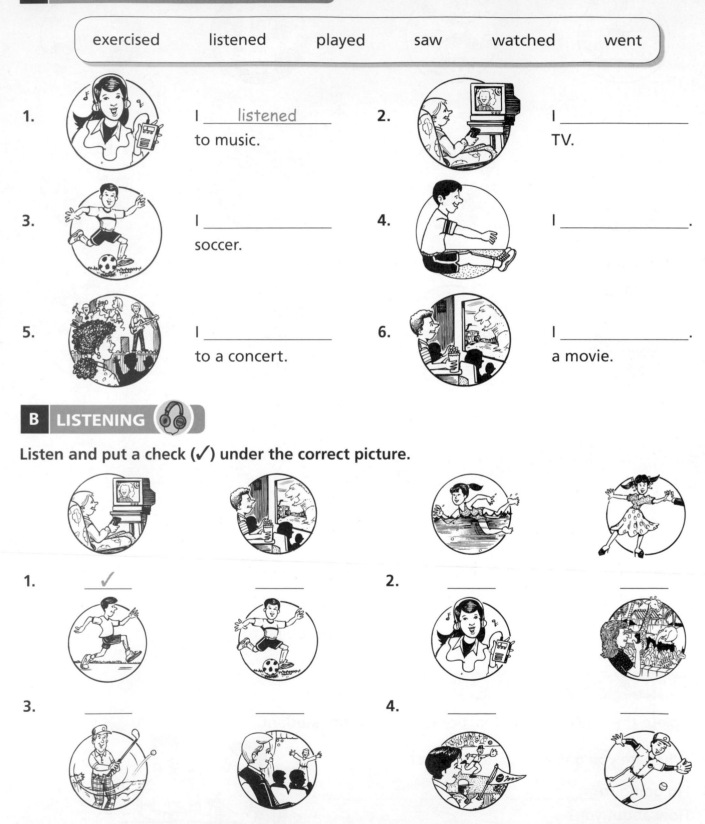

| exercised | listened | played | saw | watched | went |

1. I ___listened___ to music.

2. I _____ TV.

3. I _____ soccer.

4. I _____.

5. I _____ to a concert.

6. I _____. a movie.

B LISTENING

Listen and put a check (✓) under the correct picture.

1. ___✓___   _____

2. _____   _____

3. _____   _____

4. _____   _____

5. _____   _____

6. _____

MATCHING

1.	I played	TV.	7. I listened to	swimming.
2.	I went to	tennis.	8. I played	soccer.
3.	I watched	a concert.	9. I went	music.

4.	I saw	the park.	10. I went	a play.
5.	I went to	baseball.	11. I played	rollerblading.
6.	I played	a movie.	12. I saw	golf.

D **WHICH ONE DOESN'T BELONG?**

1.	played soccer	played golf	exercised	played tennis
2.	went to a ballgame	listened to music	went to a museum	went to a concert
3.	went swimming	went to the zoo	saw a play	watched TV
4.	went to the museum	saw a play	went to the park	saw a movie
5.	saw a play	watched TV	saw a movie	went jogging

E **LAST WEEKEND**

Tell about yourself.

	Yes, I did.	No, I didn't.
1. Did you see a movie last weekend?	_____	_____
2. Did you see a play last weekend?	_____	_____
3. Did you watch TV last weekend?	_____	_____
4. Did you go swimming last weekend?	_____	_____
5. Did you go to a concert last weekend?	_____	_____
6. Did you go to the park last weekend?	_____	_____
7. Did you exercise last weekend?	_____	_____

A MATCHING

June

Sunday	Monday	Tuesday	Wednesday	Thursday	Friday	Saturday
			1 WORK	**2** WORK	**3** WORK	**4** BASKETBALL
5 TENNIS	**6** WORK JOGGING	**7** WORK EXERCISE	**8** WORK JOGGING	**9** WORK EXERCISE	**10** WORK JOGGING	**11** CONCERT: DAVIS HALL
12 TENNIS	**13** WORK JOGGING	**14** WORK EXERCISE	**15** WORK JOGGING	**16** WORK EXERCISE	**17** WORK JOGGING	**18** BASKETBALL
19 TENNIS	**20** WORK JOGGING	**21** WORK EXERCISE	**22** WORK JOGGING	**23** WORK EXERCISE	**24** WORK JOGGING	**25** PLAY: IVY THEATER
26 TENNIS	**27** WORK JOGGING	**28** WORK EXERCISE	**29** WORK JOGGING	**30** WORK EXERCISE		

1. Carmen works   twice a week.

2. She goes jogging   on the 4th Saturday in June.

3. She exercises   twice a month.

4. She plays tennis   five days a week.

5. She plays basketball   on the 2nd Saturday in June.

6. She's going to go to a concert   three times a week.

7. She's going to go to a play   once a week.

B LISTENING

Listen and circle the words you hear.

1. four days   (five days)   4. May 7th   May 11th

2. once   twice   5. August 1st   August 4th

3. two times   three times   6. 1st Friday   3rd Friday

A MATCHING

1. What do you do?	I saw a play.
2. Tell me about your job skills.	Down the hall.
3. What did you do yesterday?	I'm an electrician.
4. Where's the personnel office?	Take the Blue Line.
5. How do I get to the mall?	I can paint.

B WHICH WORD?

1. I'm looking for a job as a (gardener   restaurant).

2. I'm an experienced (mailroom   truck driver).

3. I (can   can't) cook, but I'm sure I can learn quickly.

4. Careful! Put on your (floor   safety glasses).

5. I'm going to see a play (tomorrow   yesterday).

6. I went to the zoo (tomorrow   yesterday).

7. Benjamin works forty hours a (day   week).

8. I like to (go   went) to the park on Saturday afternoon.

9. Walk that way. The clinic is on the (right   right turn).

C LISTENING

Listen and circle the words you hear.

1.	baker	painter	4. go dancing	go jogging
2.	can	can't	5. play	played
3.	Bus Number 17	Bus Number 7	6. twice	once

WORKBOOK PAGES 1–2

A. WHAT'S THE WORD?

1. Hello
2. name
3. Hi
4. meet
5. Nice
6. you

B. WHAT'S THE WORD?

1. My
2. is
3. Hello
4. I'm
5. to
6. you

C. FIRST OR LAST?

1. last
2. first
3. first
4. last

D. WHAT'S THE LETTER?

1. C
2. E
3. G
4. L
5. M
6. Q
7. T
8. V
9. Z

E. WHAT'S THE LETTER?

1. B
2. M
3. D
4. A
5. T
6. H
7. O
8. R
9. F
10. Z
11. J
12. V

F. LISTENING

Listen and circle the word you hear.

1. Hello. My name is Yoko Morita.
2. My first name is Yoko.
3. My last name is Morita.
4. I'm Fernando Lopez.
5. Nice to meet you.
6. Nice meeting you, too.

Answers

1. Hello
2. first
3. last
4. I'm
5. you
6. Nice

WORKBOOK PAGES 3–4

A. WHAT'S THE ANSWER?

1. Veronica.
2. Gomez.
3. V-E-R-O-N-I-C-A.
4. G-O-M-E-Z.

B. MISSING LETTERS

Missing Letters: E, J, P, U, Y

C. MISSING LETTERS AND WORDS

Missing Letters:

C, E, I, N
O, T
E, M, T
O, U, Y

N I C E   T O   M E E T   Y O U

D. LISTENING

Listen and write the missing letters.

1. A. What's your last name?
   B. Watson.
   A. How do you spell it?
   B. W-A-T-S-O-N.

2. A. What's your first name?
   B. Daniel.
   A. How do you spell it?
   B. D-A-N-I-E-L.

3. A. What's your first name?
   B. Gloria.
   A. How do you spell it?
   B. G-L-O-R-I-A.

4. A. What's your last name?
   B. Peterson.
   A. How do you spell it?
   B. P-E-T-E-R-S-O-N.

5. A. What's your first name?
   B. Roger.
   A. How do you spell it?
   B. R-O-G-E-R.

6. A. What's your last name?
   B. Young.
   A. How do you spell it?
   B. Y-O-U-N-G.

7. A. What's your last name?
   B. Montero.
   A. How do you spell it?
   B. M-O-N-T-E-R-O.

8. A. What's your last name?
   B. Figueroa.
   A. How do you spell it?
   B. F-I-G-U-E-R-O-A.

Answers

1. W A T S O N
2. D A N I E L
3. G L O R I A
4. P E T E R S O N
5. R O G E R
6. Y O U N G
7. M O N T E R O
8. F I G U E R O A

E. CROSSWORD

(See page 153.)

WORKBOOK PAGES 5–6

A. WRITE THE NUMBERS

nine	one	three
five	seven	eight
two	ten	six
four	zero	

B. CROSSWORD

(See page 153.)

C. LISTENING

Listen and write the numbers you hear.

1. A. What's your telephone number?
   B. 261–5824.
   A. Is that 261–5824?
   B. Yes. That's correct.

2. A. What's your telephone number?
   B. 975–5864.
   A. Is that 975–5864?
   B. Yes. That's correct.

3. A. What's your telephone number?
   B. 832–7144.
   A. Is that 832–7144?
   B. Yes. That's correct.

4. A. What's your telephone number?
   B. 537–6704.
   A. Is that 537–6704?
   B. Yes. That's correct.

5. A. What's your telephone number?
   B. 961–4208.
   A. Is that 961–4208?
   B. Yes. That's correct.

6. A. What's your telephone number?
   B. 777–8241.
   A. Is that 777–8241?
   B. Yes. That's correct.

7. A. What's your telephone number?
   B. 421–9075.
   A. Is that 421–9075?
   B. Yes. That's correct.

8. A. What's your telephone number?
   B. 640–7401.
   A. Is that 640–7401?
   B. Yes. That's correct.

9. A. What's your telephone number?
   B. 353–1165.
   A. Is that 353–1165?
   B. Yes. That's correct.

10. A. What's your telephone number?
    B. 462–5096.
    A. Is that 462–5096?
    B. Yes. That's correct.

11. A. What's your telephone number?
    B. 277–4949.
    A. Is that 277–4949?
    B. Yes. That's correct.

12. A. What's your telephone number?
    B. 668–5033.
    A. Is that 668–5033?
    B. Yes. That's correct.

Answers

1. 2 6 1 – 5 8 2 4
2. 9 7 5 – 5 8 6 4
3. 8 3 2 – 7 1 4 4
4. 5 3 7 – 6 7 0 4
5. 9 6 1 – 4 2 0 8
6. 7 7 7 – 8 2 4 1
7. 4 2 1 – 9 0 7 5
8. 6 4 0 – 7 4 0 1
9. 3 5 3 – 1 1 6 5
10. 4 6 2 – 5 0 9 6
11. 2 7 7 – 4 9 4 9
12. 6 6 8 – 5 0 3 3

D. NUMBER SEARCH

(See page 153.)

E. WRITE THE NUMBERS

1. three
2. five
3. one
4. two
5. four
6. nine

WORKBOOK PAGES 7–8

A. WHAT'S THE WORD?

1. What's
2. address
3. Street
4. say
5. 9

B. WHAT'S THE WORD?

1. My
2. number
3. you
4. say
5. No

C. WHAT'S THE ANSWER?

1. Ronald.
2. Harrison.
3. 5 River Street.
4. No. 5 River Street.
5. 4C.
6. 289–3705.

D. LISTENING

Listen and write the information.

A. What's your first name?
B. Bernardo.
A. How do you spell it?
B. B-E-R-N-A-R-D-O.
A. Is that B-E-R-N-A-R-D-O?
B. Yes. That's correct.

A. What's your last name?
B. Ortiz.
A. How do you spell it?
B. O-R-T-I-Z.
A. Is that O-R-T-I-Z?
B. Yes. That's correct.

A. What's your address?
B. 5 Rowley Street.
A. Did you say 9?
B. No. 5.
A. How do you spell Rowley?
B. R-O-W-L-E-Y.
A. Is that R-O-W-L-E-Y?
B. Yes. That's correct.

A. What's your apartment number?
B. My apartment number is 4C.
A. Did you say 4D?
B. No. 4C.

A. What's the name of your city?
B. Easterly.

A. How do you spell it?
B. E-A-S-T-E-R-L-Y.
A. Is that E-A-S-T-E-R-L-Y ?
B. Yes. That's correct. Easterly, New Mexico.
A. What's the abbreviation of New Mexico?
B. NM.

A. What's your zip code?
B. 10375.
A. Is that 10375?
B. Yes. That's correct.

A. And what's your area code?
B. 629.
A. Did you say 692?
B. No. 629.

A. And your telephone number?
B. 791–2864.
A. Is that 791–2864?
B. Yes. That's correct.
A. So that's 629–791–2864?
B. Yes. That's correct.

Answers

(See page 154.)

WORKBOOK PAGE 9

A. WHO ARE THEY?

1. son
2. brother
3. mother
4. husband
5. grandfather
6. granddaughter
7. aunt
8. nephew

B. LISTENING

Listen and circle the word you hear.

1. A. This is my daughter.
   B. Nice to meet you.

2. A. This is my mother.
   B. Nice to meet you.

3. A. This is my husband.
   B. Nice to meet you.

4. A. This is my grandmother.
   B. Nice to meet you.

5. A. This is my niece.
   B. Nice to meet you.

6. A. This is my grandson.
   B. Nice to meet you.

Answers

1. daughter
2. mother
3. husband
4. grandmother
5. niece
6. grandson

WORKBOOK PAGE 10

A. WHICH WORD?

1. daughter	6. son
2. her	7. his
3. Her	8. His
4. she	9. he
5. She's	10. He's

B. WHAT'S THE WORD?

1. He's	4. His
2. She's	5. Who, is
3. This	6. your, old

WORKBOOK PAGE 11

A. WHAT'S THE WORD?

1. pen	5. ruler
2. eraser	6. notebook
3. book	7. calculator
4. pencil	

B. LISTENING

Listen and circle the word you hear.

1. A. Is this your pencil?
   B. Yes, it is.
2. A. Is this your ruler?
   B. No, it isn't.
3. A. Is this your book?
   B. Yes, it is.
4. A. Where's the calculator?
   B. Over there.
5. A. Is this your pen?
   B. No, it isn't.
6. A. Where's the eraser?
   B. Over there.

Answers

1. pencil	4. calculator
2. ruler	5. pen
3. book	6. eraser

WORKBOOK PAGES 12–13

A. MATCHING

1. desk
2. globe
3. board
4. overhead projector
5. chalk
6. bookshelf
7. TV
8. map
9. bulletin board
10. computer

B. WHERE ARE THEY?

1. c	5. d
2. f	6. a
3. b	7. h
4. e	8. g

WORKBOOK PAGE 14

A. WHAT'S THE WORD?

1. There's	5. There's
2. There are	6. There are
3. There are	7. There are
4. There's	8. There's

B. MATCHING

1. computer in my classroom.
2. overhead projector in my classroom.
3. a globe in my classroom.
4. calculators in my classroom.
5. my classroom.

C. LISTENING

Listen and circle the word you hear.

1. There are pencils on the bookshelf.
2. There's an eraser on my desk.
3. There's an overhead projector next to the bookshelf.
4. There are students in my classroom.
5. There's a map on the bulletin board.
6. There are erasers on my desk.

Answers

1. pencils	4. There are
2. desk	5. on
3. an	6. are

WORKBOOK PAGES 15–16

A. CHOOSE THE CORRECT ACTION

1. a	4. b
2. b	5. b
3. b	6. a

B. WHICH WORD?

1. Stand	4. Put away
2. Raise	5. Sit
3. Go	

C. LISTENING

Listen and circle the word you hear.

1. Open your book.
2. Raise your hand.
3. Take out your book.
4. Stand up.
5. Write your name.
6. Go to the board.

Answers

1. Open	4. Stand
2. Raise	5. Write
3. Take out	6. Go

E. LISTENING

Listen and circle the correct answer.

1. Is there a screen in the classroom?
2. Is there a TV in the classroom?
3. Is there a bookshelf in the classroom?
4. Is there a globe in the classroom?
5. Is there a computer in the classroom?
6. Is there a board in the classroom?
7. Is there a bulletin board in the classroom?
8. Is there chalk in the classroom?

Answers

1. Yes, there is.
2. Yes, there is.
3. No, there isn't.
4. No, there isn't.
5. Yes, there is.
6. Yes, there is.
7. No, there isn't.
8. Yes, there is.

WORKBOOK PAGE 17

A. MATCHING

1. fourteen   5. fifteen
2. nineteen   6. eleven
3. seventeen   7. eighteen
4. thirteen   8. twelve

B. LISTENING

Listen and circle the number you hear.

1. There are fourteen students in my English class.
2. There are eleven students in my English class.
3. There are twelve students in my English class.
4. There are nineteen students in my English class.
5. There are fifteen students in my English class.
6. There are seventeen students in my English class.

Answers

1. 14   4. 19
2. 11   5. 15
3. 12   6. 17

C. NUMBER SEARCH

(See page 154.)

WORKBOOK PAGES 18–20

A. EVERY DAY

1. watch TV
2. comb my hair
3. get up
4. eat breakfast
5. brush my teeth
6. read
7. come home
8. get undressed
9. go to bed
10. cook dinner
11. get dressed
12. take a shower

B. WHAT DO YOU DO?

1. b   4. b
2. a   5. b
3. b   6. a

C. LISTENING

Listen and write the number under the correct picture.

1. Every day I comb my hair.
2. Every day I eat lunch.
3. Every day I take a shower.
4. Every day I go to work.
5. Every day I get up.
6. Every day I get dressed.
7. Every day I go to school.
8. Every day I watch TV.
9. Every day I come home.

Answers

2	7	9
8	1	4
6	5	3

D. CROSSWORD

(See page 154.)

WORKBOOK PAGES 21–22

A. CHOOSE THE CORRECT ACTIVITY

1. b   4. a
2. a   5. b
3. b   6. a

B. LISTENING

Listen and write the number under the correct picture.

1. A. What are you doing?
   B. I'm making breakfast.

2. A. What are you doing?
   B. I'm washing the dishes.

3. A. What are you doing?
   B. I'm cleaning.

4. A. What are you doing?
   B. I'm reading.

5. A. What are you doing?
   B. I'm watching TV.

6. A. What are you doing?
   B. I'm combing my hair.

Answers

5	6	1
2	3	4

C. WHICH WORD?

1. making   4. feeding
2. watching   5. dishes
3. doing

D. WHAT'S THE WORD?

1. watching   4. doing
2. feeding   5. playing
3. making   6. listening

WORKBOOK PAGES 23–24

A. MATCHING

1. cooks dinner every day.
2. cooking dinner right now.
3. cook dinner every day.
4. listen to music every day.
5. listening to music right now.
6. listens to music every day.
7. watches TV every day.
8. watch TV every day.
9. watching TV right now.
10. going to work right now.
11. goes to work every day.
12. go to work every day.

B. EVERY DAY OR RIGHT NOW?

1. I clean
2. I'm eating
3. I wash
4. I'm playing
5. I go
6. I'm getting
7. I'm listening
8. I brush
9. I'm watching
10. I'm feeding
11. I do
12. I take

D. LISTENING

Listen and circle the sentence you hear.

1. I'm cleaning the house.
2. I make breakfast.
3. I feed the baby.
4. I'm reading.
5. I'm studying.
6. I'm ironing.
7. I comb my hair.
8. I eat lunch.
9. I do the laundry.
10. I'm watching TV.

Answers

1. a   6. b
2. b   7. b
3. b   8. a
4. b   9. b
5. a   10. b

WORKBOOK PAGES 25–26

A. MATCHING

1. It's raining.
2. It's sunny.
3. It's cloudy.

4. It's snowing.
5. It's hot.
6. It's cold.
7. It's foggy.

B. LISTENING

Listen and circle the word you hear.

1. A. What's the weather?
   B. It's sunny.

2. A. What's the weather?
   B. It's raining.

3. A. What's the weather?
   B. It's cold.

4. A. What's the weather?
   B. It's foggy.

5. A. What's the weather?
   B. It's cloudy.

6. A. What's the weather?
   B. It's hot.

Answers

1. sunny	4. foggy
2. raining	5. cloudy
3. cold	6. hot

C. WORD SEARCH

(See page 154.)

D. WHAT'S THE WEATHER?

1. foggy	5. snowing
2. cloudy	6. cold
3. sunny	7. hot
4. raining	

WORKBOOK PAGE 27

A. MATCHING

1. 40	6. 54
2. 35	7. 100
3. 70	8. 90
4. 66	9. 81
5. 22	10. 47

B. WHAT'S THE NUMBER?

1. 30	6. 89
2. 60	7. 91
3. 53	8. 26
4. 75	9. 58
5. 43	10. 62

C. WHAT'S THE WORD?

1. twenty
2. eighty

3. thirty-six
4. forty-nine
5. fifty-seven
6. sixty-three
7. seventy-eight
8. eighty-four
9. ninety-two
10. twenty-one

D. LISTENING

Listen and circle the number you hear.

1. A. How old are you?
   B. I'm sixty years old.

2. A. How old is your son?
   B. He's twenty-one years old.

3. A. What's your address?
   B. Forty-four Main Street.

4. A. What's the temperature?
   B. It's seventy-two degrees.

5. A. How old is your grandmother?
   B. She's sixty-nine years old.

6. A. How old is your mother?
   B. She's fifty-four years old.

7. A. What's your address?
   B. Eighty-nine Center Street.

8. A. What's the temperature?
   B. It's forty-four degrees.

9. A. What's your address?
   B. Thirty-three Franklin Street.

Answers

1. 60	6. 54
2. 21	7. 89
3. 44	8. 44
4. 72	9. 33
5. 69	

WORKBOOK PAGE 28

A. MATCHING

1. It's raining.
2. I'm cooking.
3. It's on the bookshelf.
4. This is my sister.
5. He's ten years old.
6. Yes, it is.

B. WHICH WORD?

1. She's	5. reading
2. an	6. apartment
3. hand	7. globes
4. shower	8. watch

C. LISTENING

Listen and circle the words you hear.

1. Hello. I'm Sylvia Montero.
2. Is this your calculator?
3. My phone number is 768–3569.
4. This is Maria. She's my cousin.
5. Open your book.
6. I'm cleaning.

Answers

1. I'm	4. cousin
2. calculator	5. open
3. 768–3569	6. cleaning

WORKBOOK PAGES 29–30

A. WHAT'S THE NUMBER?

seventy
twenty
thirteen
eighty

sixteen
one hundred
thirty-three
eleven

fifty
forty
nineteen
sixty

B. WHAT'S THE ANSWER?

1. nine	4. thirty-four
2. five	5. fifty
3. fifteen	

C. WHAT'S THE ORDER?

1. 2		3. 3	
3		2	
1		1	
2. 2		4. 1	
3		3	
1		2	

D. CROSSWORD

(See page 154.)

E. LISTENING

Listen and circle the number you hear.

1. My address is thirteen fifty-five Main Street.
2. My address is six ninety-seven Main Street.
3. My address is thirty-four nineteen River Street.
4. My address is forty-one seventy-four Center Street.
5. My address is seventeen ninety Pine Street.
6. I'm in Apartment five oh nine.
7. I'm in Apartment one fourteen.
8. My English class is in Room eight eighty.
9. My English class is in Room two twenty-three.
10. My English class is in Room one oh one.

Answers

1. 1355 Main Street
2. 697 Main Street
3. 3419 River Street
4. 4174 Center Street
5. 1790 Pine Street
6. Apartment 509
7. Apartment 114
8. Room 880
9. Room 223
10. Room 101

WORKBOOK PAGE 31

A. MATCHING

1. It's four o'clock.
2. It's twelve o'clock.
3. It's eight fifteen.
4. It's six thirty.
5. It's three forty-five.
6. It's eight thirty.
7. It's four forty-five.
8. It's two fifteen.
9. It's five o'clock.
10. It's seven thirty.

B. LISTENING

Listen and put a check under the time you hear.

1. It's eleven o'clock.
2. It's four fifteen.
3. It's five thirty.
4. It's ten forty-five.
5. It's seven thirty.
6. It's eleven forty-five.

Answers

1. ___ ✓
2. ___ ✓
3. ✓ ___
4. ✓ ___
5. ___ ✓
6. ✓ ___

WORKBOOK PAGES 32–33

A. DAYS OF THE WEEK WORD SEARCH

(See page 154.)

B. WHAT'S THE ORDER?

4 3
7 1
2 5
6

C. LISTENING

Listen and circle the word you hear.

1. A. What day is it?
   B. It's Tuesday.

2. A. What day is it?
   B. It's Friday.

3. A. Can you come in today at nine thirty?
   B. Yes, I can.

4. A. What day is it?
   B. It's Thursday.

5. A. Can you come in today at two fifteen?
   B. Yes, I can.

6. A. What day is it?
   B. It's Sunday.

Answers

1. Tuesday
2. Friday
3. 9:30
4. Thursday
5. 2:15
6. Sunday

D. WHAT'S THE LETTER?

1. T H U R S <u>D</u> A Y
2. S <u>A</u> T U R D A Y
3. M <u>O</u> N D A <u>Y</u>
4. T U E <u>S</u> D A Y
5. <u>F</u> R I D A Y
6. W <u>E</u> D N E <u>S</u> D A Y

E. WHAT'S THE DAY?

1. Tuesday
2. Thursday
3. Wednesday
4. Friday
5. Monday
6. Saturday
7. Sunday

WORKBOOK PAGES 34–35

A. WHICH FLOOR?

1. 10th
2. 16th
3. 2nd
4. 77th
5. 40th
6. 15th
7. 13th
8. 80th

B. WHAT'S THE NUMBER?

third   sixth   nineteenth
ninth   ninetieth   eighth
fourth   twelfth   first

C. LISTENING

Listen and circle the number you hear.

1. A. What floor do you live on?
   B. I live on the seventeenth floor.
   A. The seventeenth?
   B. Yes.

2. A. What floor do you live on?
   B. I live on the sixth floor.
   A. The sixth?
   B. Yes.

3. A. What floor do you live on?
   B. I live on the eleventh floor.
   A. The eleventh?
   B. Yes.

4. A. Is this the fifth floor?
   B. Yes, it is.

5. A. What floor do you live on?
   B. I live on the thirty-third floor.
   A. The thirty-third floor?
   B. Yes.

6. A. What floor is this?
   B. The eighth.
   A. The eighth?
   B. Yes.

7. A. Is this the forty-second floor?
   B. Yes, it is.

8. A. What floor do you live on?
    B. I live on the fifteenth floor.
    A. The fifteenth?
    B. Yes, that's right.

9. A. What floor is this?
    B. It's the fortieth.
    A. The fortieth? Thanks.

10. A. Is this the sixteenth floor?
    B. Yes, it is.

11. A. What floor do you live on?
    B. I live on the nineteenth floor.
    A. The nineteenth?
    B. Yes.

12. A. Excuse me. Is this the fifty-fourth floor?
    B. Yes, it is.

Answers

1. 17th	7. 42nd
2. 6th	8. 15th
3. 11th	9. 40th
4. 5th	10. 16th
5. 33rd	11. 19th
6. 8th	12. 54th

D. CROSSWORD

(See page 154.)

WORKBOOK PAGES 36–37

A. WHAT'S THE MONTH?

(See page 154.)

B. LISTENING

Listen and circle the month you hear.

1. A. What month is it?
    B. It's September.
    A. Thanks.

2. A. What month is it?
    B. It's November.
    A. Thanks.

3. A. What month is it?
    B. It's January.
    A. Thanks.

4. A. What month is it?
    B. It's April.
    A. Thanks.

5. A. What month is it?
    B. It's May.
    A. Thanks.

6. A. What month is it?
    B. It's July.
    A. Thanks.

Answers

1. September	4. April
2. November	5. May
3. January	6. July

C. WHAT'S THE ORDER?

2	7
12	11
10	6
9	1
8	3
4	5

D. MATCHING

1. It's Tuesday.
2. It's May.
3. It's December 10, 2012.
4. It's two fifteen.

F. LISTENING

Listen and circle the correct answer.

1. A. When is your birthday?
    B. My birthday is November ninth.

2. A. When is your birthday?
    B. My birthday is August first.

3. A. What's today's date?
    B. It's June eleventh, two thousand twelve.

4. A. What's today's date?
    B. It's January fifteenth, two thousand twelve.

5. A. I go to work from nine to five.
    B. From nine to five?
    A. Yes.

6. A. When do you go to school?
    B. From eight-thirty to three.
    A. From eight-thirty to three?
    B. Yes.

Answers

1. November 9th
2. August 1st

3. June 11, 2012
4. January 15, 2012
5. from 9 to 5
6. from 8:30 to 3

WORKBOOK PAGES 38–39

A. WHAT'S THE COIN?

1. nickel	4. penny
2. dime	5. half dollar
3. quarter	

B. MATCHING

1. $.25	4. 5¢
2. $.10	5. 50¢
3. $.01	6. 25¢

C. HOW MUCH MONEY?

1. fifteen dollars
2. twenty-two dollars
3. nine dollars
4. thirty dollars
5. thirty dollars
6. sixty-six dollars

D. MATCHING

1. $11.25	4. $55.01
2. $5.25	5. $5.86
3. $21.50	

E. WHICH ONE DOESN'T BELONG?

1. fifteen cents
2. $25
3. $10
4. nickel
5. 50¢
6. $.10
7. $.20

WORKBOOK PAGE 40

A. MATCHING

1. 6	6. 45th
2. 16th	7. 54
3. 60	8. 1515
4. 60th	9. $15.50
5. 1660	10. 5:15

B. WHICH WORD?

1. fourteen	5. 9:30
2. thirty	6. fourth
3. 245	7. eleven
4. third	8. tenth

C. WHICH ONE DOESN'T BELONG?

1. sixteenth (The others are cardinal numbers.)
2. 5:00 (The others are amounts of money.)
3. $6.45 (The others are times.)
4. seven (The others are ordinal numbers.)
5. 3:15 (The others are hour times.)

D. LISTENING

Listen and circle the correct numbers.

1. Nineteen plus nine is twenty-eight.
2. My address is 320 Jefferson Street.
3. Can you come in on Friday at ten thirty?
4. What's the third month of the year?
5. I live on the fourteenth floor.
6. My birthday is August eleventh.
7. I just found two dollars!
8. I work from nine to five.
9. Today's date is June sixth, two thousand ten.

Answers

1.	28	6.	11th
2.	320	7.	$2.00
3.	10:30	8.	9 to 5
4.	3rd	9.	6th
5.	14th		

WORKBOOK PAGE 41

A. WHAT'S THE WORD?

1. living room
2. kitchen
3. bathroom
4. bedroom
5. dining room
6. patio
7. balcony

B. LISTENING

Listen and circle the word you hear.

1. A. Tell me about the apartment.
   B. It has a very nice living room.
2. A. Tell me about the apartment.
   B. It has a very nice bathroom.
3. A. Tell me about the apartment.
   B. It has a very nice dining room.
4. A. Tell me about the apartment.
   B. It has a very nice balcony.
5. A. Tell me about the apartment.
   B. It has a very nice bedroom.
6. A. Tell me about the apartment.
   B. It has a very nice kitchen.

Answers

1. living room
2. bathroom
3. dining room
4. balcony
5. bedroom
6. kitchen

WORKBOOK PAGES 42–43

A. WHAT'S THE WORD?

1. fireplace
2. refrigerator
3. stove
4. closet
5. shower
6. window

B. WHICH WORD?

1. shower   3. stove
2. closet   4. fireplace

C. WORD SEARCH

(See page 154.)

D. LISTENING

Listen and write the number under the correct picture.

1. There's a stove in the kitchen.
2. Is there a dining room in the apartment?
3. There's a closet in the bedroom.
4. There's a very nice balcony.
5. There's a refrigerator in the kitchen.
6. Is there a fireplace in the apartment?
7. There's a nice patio.
8. There's a window in the bathroom.
9. There's a very nice living room in the apartment.

Answers

6	1	9
5	3	8
7	2	4

WORKBOOK PAGES 44–45

A. MATCHING

1. sofa   5. lamp
2. table   6. rug
3. picture   7. bed
4. chair

B. LISTENING

Listen and circle the word you hear.

1. Put the bed over there.
2. Put the sofa over there.
3. Put the chair in the living room.
4. Put the picture in the kitchen.
5. Put the table in the living room.
6. Put the lamp on the patio.

Answers

1. bed   4. picture
2. sofa   5. table
3. living room 6. lamp

C. YES OR NO?

1. Yes, there is.
2. Yes, there is.
3. No, there isn't.
4. Yes, there is.
5. Yes, there is.
6. No, there isn't.
7. No, there isn't.
8. Yes, there is.
9. No, there isn't.
10. Yes, there is.
11. No, there isn't.

WORKBOOK PAGE 46

A. WHAT'S THE ANSWER?

1. There are four floors.
2. There are eight apartments.

3. There are four rooms.
4. There's one closet.
5. There are five cabinets.
6. There are two windows.

B. WHICH WORD?

1. Tenth
2. four
3. third
4. two

A. WHAT'S THE WORD?

1. clinic
2. bakery
3. bus station
4. drug store
5. bank
6. gas station
7. library
8. laundromat
9. grocery store

C. LISTENING

Listen and put a check under the place you hear.

1. A. Where are you going?
   B. I'm going to the bakery.

2. A. Where are you going?
   B. I'm going to the drug store.

3. A. Where are you going?
   B. I'm going to the bus station.

4. A. Where are you going?
   B. I'm going to the laundromat.

Answers

1. __ ✓
2. ✓ __
3. __ ✓
4. ✓ __

D. WORD SEARCH

(See page 155.)

A. MATCHING

1. i
2. a
3. j
4. b
5. f
6. d
7. g
8. c
9. e
10. h

C. WHICH PLACE DOESN'T BELONG?

1. movie theater (The others are places where people buy food.)
2. shopping mall (The others are related to transportation.)
3. bank (The others are places where people buy food.)
4. park (The others are medical places.)
5. post office (The others are places where people shop.)

D. LISTENING

Listen and put a check under the two places you hear.

1. A. Where are you going?
   B. I'm going to the bank, and then I'm going to the post office.

2. A. Where are you going?
   B. I'm going to the department store, and then I'm going to the supermarket.

3. A. Where are you going?
   B. I'm going to the library. How about you?
   A. I'm going to the laundromat.

4. A. Where are you going?
   B. I'm going to the park. How about you?
   A. I'm going to the zoo.

Answers

1. ✓ __ ✓
2. __ ✓ ✓
3. ✓ __ ✓
4. ✓ __ ✓

A. WHERE ARE THEY?

1. a
2. a
3. b
4. a
5. b
6. a
7. b

B. WHICH WORD?

1. on
2. next to
3. across from
4. between
5. on
6. across from

C. LISTENING

Listen and write the number under the correct picture.

1. There's a clinic on Main Street, across from the post office.
2. There's a clinic on Pine Street, next to the laundromat.
3. There's a library on Center Street, between the post office and the park.
4. There's a library on Central Avenue, between the post office and the bank.
5. There's a grocery store on Pine Street, next to the bakery.
6. There's a grocery store on Main Street, across from the bakery.

Answers

| 3 | 5 | 1 |
| 6 | 2 | 4 |

A. WHAT'S THE WORD?

1. across from
2. next to
3. on
4. between
5. next to
6. on
7. between
8. across from

B. LISTENING

Listen and write the names of the places on the map.

1. There's a library on Ninth Avenue, between the clinic and the department store.
2. There's a movie theater on Center Street, across from the train station.
3. There's a park on Center Street, next to the post office.
4. There's a restaurant on Pine Street, next to the bank.
5. There's a shopping mall on Tenth Avenue, between the drug store and the bank.

6. There's a bakery on Center Street, next to the movie theater and across from the post office.

Answers

(See page 155.)

C. WHICH WORD?

1. Eleventh
2. three
3. Sixth
4. Second
5. Thirteenth
6. four, Eighth

WORKBOOK PAGE 55

A. MATCHING

1. It's September.
2. It's Saturday.
3. It's seven thirty.
4. It's on State Street.
5. Yes, there is.

B. WHAT'S THE WORD?

1. shower
2. kitchen
3. closets
4. chair
5. laundromat

C. WHICH WORD?

1. second
2. stove
3. across from
4. Main Street

D. LISTENING

Listen and circle the words you hear.

1. I live at 1519 Center Street.
2. It's 7:30.
3. The bus station is on Main Street.
4. I live on the fourth floor.
5. Can you come in on Tuesday at one forty-five?
6. Put this table in the dining room.

Answers

1. 1519
2. 7:30
3. bus station
4. fourth
5. Tuesday
6. dining room

WORKBOOK PAGE 56

A. CHOOSE

1. young
2. old
3. middle-aged
4. short
5. tall
6. average height

B. WHICH WORD?

1. short
2. old
3. young
4. tall
5. middle-aged
6. average height

C. LISTENING

Listen and circle the word you hear.

1. A. What's her age?
   B. She's young.

2. A. What's his height?
   B. He's tall.

3. A. What's her height?
   B. She's short.

4. A. What's his age?
   B. He's middle-aged.

5. A. What's her height?
   B. She's average height.

6. A. What's their age?
   B. They're old.

Answers

1. young
2. tall
3. short
4. middle-aged
5. average height
6. old

WORKBOOK PAGES 57–58

A. WHICH WORD?

1. black
2. blond
3. blue
4. has
5. have
6. have
7. gray, blue

B. MISSING LETTERS

1. b l u e
2. b l a c k

3. r e d, b r o w n
4. g r e e n
5. w h i t e
6. g r a y

C. LISTENING

Listen and circle the word you hear.

1. He has brown hair.
2. She has green eyes.
3. They have blue eyes.
4. He has white hair.
5. I have blond hair.
6. You have black eyes.

Answers

1. brown
2. green
3. blue
4. white
5. blond
6. black

D. WHAT'S THE WORD?

1. tall, hair
2. short, straight black
3. height, curly

E. LISTENING

Listen and put a check under the correct person.

1. A. What does he look like?
   B. He's short, with black hair.

2. A. What does she look like?
   B. She's tall, with curly brown hair.

3. A. What does he look like?
   B. He's tall and heavy.

4. A. What does she look like?
   B. She's short, with straight black hair.

5. A. What does he look like?
   B. He's average height, with gray hair.

6. A. What does she look like?
   B. She's average height, with black hair.

Answers

1. ___ ✓
2. ✓ ___
3. ___ ✓
4. ✓ ___
5. ___ ✓
6. ✓ ___

A. MATCHING

1. He's single.
2. They're married.
3. She's widowed.
4. I'm divorced.

B. WHAT'S THE WORD?

1. hungry	5. afraid
2. sick	6. happy
3. angry	7. sad
4. thirsty	8. tired

C. LISTENING

Listen and put a check under the correct picture.

1. A. Are you hungry?
   B. Yes. I'm very hungry.

2. A. Are you happy?
   B. Yes. I'm very happy.

3. A. Are you sick?
   B. Yes. I'm very sick.

4. A. Are you angry?
   B. Yes. I'm very angry.

Answers

1. ___ ✓
2. ✓ ___
3. ✓ ___
4. ✓ ___

D. WORD SEARCH

(See page 155.)

A. MATCHING

1. Haiti.
   Haitian.
2. Vietnam.
   Vietnamese.
3. Japan.
   Japanese.
4. Greece.
   Greek.
5. Brazil.
   Portuguese.
6. China.
   Chinese.
7. Mexico.
   Spanish.
8. Korea.
   Korean.
9. Russia.
   Russian.

10. Morocco.
    Arabic.

B. WHICH WORD?

1. Mexico
2. Russian
3. Brazil
4. Japan
5. Greece, Greek

C. LISTENING

Listen and circle the word you hear.

1. I'm from Mexico.
2. I speak Haitian.
3. I'm from China.
4. I speak Japanese.
5. I'm from Korea.
6. I speak Russian.
7. I speak Vietnamese.
8. I'm from Brazil.
9. I speak Greek.

Answers

1. Mexico	6. Russian
2. Haitian	7. Vietnamese
3. China	8. Brazil
4. Japanese	9. Greek
5. Korea	

A. WHAT'S THE WORD?

1. young
2. pounds
3. short
4. middle-aged
5. weight
6. young
7. height

B. WHICH WORD?

1. six	4. pounds
2. fifty	5. old
3. feet	

C. LISTENING

Listen and circle the words you hear.

1. A. How tall are you?
   B. I'm five feet nine inches.

2. A. How much do you weigh?
   B. I weigh a hundred and thirty pounds.

3. A. Is your brother heavy?
   B. He's average weight.

4. A. How tall are you?
   B. I'm six feet tall.

5. A. Is your sister tall?
   B. She's average height.

6. A. How tall are you?
   B. I'm six feet five inches tall.

7. A. How old is your son?
   B. He's eight years old.

8. A. How much do you weigh?
   B. I weigh ninety-nine pounds.

Answers

1. 5 feet 9 inches
2. 130 pounds
3. weight
4. tall
5. height
6. 6 feet 5 inches
7. eight
8. 99 pounds

A. MATCHING

1. orange	6. onion
2. carrot	7. tomato
3. egg	8. peach
4. banana	9. cookie
5. apple	10. potato

B. WHAT'S THE LETTER?

1. p o t a t o
2. b a n a n a
3. o n i o n
4. c o o k i e s
5. o r a n g e
6. a p p l e
7. c a r r o t s
8. e g g s
9. t o m a t o
10. p e a c h

C. LISTENING

Listen and put a check under the food you hear.

1. There aren't any more bananas.
2. I'm looking for a tomato.
3. There aren't any more onions.
4. I'm looking for an egg.
5. There aren't any more carrots.
6. I'm looking for an orange.
7. There aren't any more apples.
8. I'm looking for cookies.

1. ___ ✓
2. ✓ ___
3. ✓ ___
4. ___ ✓
5. ✓ ___
6. ✓ ___
7. ___ ✓
8. ___ ✓

WORKBOOK PAGES 65–66

A. MATCHING

1. bread
2. milk
3. lettuce
4. soda
5. butter
6. soup
7. flour
8. ice cream
9. cheese
10. cereal

B. WHAT'S THE ANSWER?

1. Yes, there is.
2. No, there aren't.
3. Yes, there is.
4. No, there isn't.
5. Yes, there are.
6. No, there aren't.
7. No, there isn't.
8. Yes, there are.
9. No, there aren't.
10. No, there isn't.
11. Yes, there are.
12. No, there isn't.

C. LISTENING

Listen and circle the word you hear.

1. I'm looking for milk.
2. I'm looking for bread.
3. I'm looking for soda.
4. I'm looking for ice cream.
5. I'm looking for potatoes.
6. I'm looking for butter.

Answers

1. milk
2. bread
3. soda
4. ice cream
5. potatoes
6. butter

WORKBOOK PAGE 67

A. WHICH WORD?

1. is
2. are
3. is
4. is
5. are
6. is

B. WHICH GROUP?

Fruits	Vegetables
apple	carrot
banana	lettuce
orange	onion
peach	potato

WORKBOOK PAGES 68–69

A. MATCHING

1. milk
2. soda
3. soup
4. bread
5. cheese
6. bananas
7. cookies
8. sugar
9. mayonnaise
10. eggs

B. LISTENING

Listen and put a check under the correct shopping list.

1. A. What do we need at the supermarket?
   B. We need a bag of flour, a can of soup, and a loaf of bread.
2. A. What do we need at the supermarket?
   B. We need a box of cookies, a pound of cheese, and a bunch of bananas.
3. A. What do we need at the supermarket?
   B. We need a bottle of soda, a bag of sugar, and a dozen apples.
4. A. What do we need at the supermarket?
   B. We need a jar of mayonnaise, oranges, and a box of cereal.

Answers

1. ___ ✓
2. ✓ ___
3. ___ ✓
4. ✓ ___

C. WORD SEARCH

(See page 155.)

WORKBOOK PAGES 70–72

A. MATCHING

1. sandwich
2. coffee
3. hamburger
4. lemonade
5. pizza
6. donut
7. hot dog
8. taco
9. cheeseburger
10. tea

B. LISTENING

Listen and circle the word you hear.

1. I'd like a hot dog, please.
2. I'd like tea, please.
3. I'd like a hamburger, please.
4. I'd like a pizza, please.
5. I'd like a taco, please.
6. I'd like lemonade, please.

Answers

1. hot dog
2. tea
3. hamburger
4. pizza
5. taco
6. lemonade

C. CROSSWORD

(See page 155.)

D. WHICH GROUP?

Things I Eat	Things I Drink
donuts	coffee
hot dogs	lemonade
pizza	milk
sandwiches	soda
tacos	tea

E. WHICH WORD?

1. milk
2. cereal
3. apples
4. peach
5. mayonnaise
6. sandwich
7. onion
8. sugar
9. quart of
10. tea

WORKBOOK PAGE 73

A. MATCHING

1. 1 lb.
2. 1 doz.
3. 1 qt.
4. 1/2 doz.
5. 1/2 lb.
6. 2 lbs.
7. 3 qts.

B. WHICH WORD?

1. butter
2. milk
3. eggs
4. potatoes
5. ice cream
6. peaches
7. apples

C. LISTENING

Listen and put a check under the correct amount.

1. Please get a quart at the supermarket.
2. Please get half a pound at the supermarket.
3. Please get two dozen at the supermarket.
4. Please get three quarts at the supermarket.

Answers

1. __ ✓
2. ✓ __
3. __ ✓
4. __ ✓

A. WHAT'S THE WORD?

1. coat
2. necklace
3. dress
4. shirt
5. umbrella
6. suit
7. sweater
8. belt
9. blouse
10. tie
11. jacket
12. watch

B. LISTENING

Listen and circle the word you hear.

1. I'm looking for a shirt.
2. Coats are over there.
3. Suits are over there.
4. I'm looking for a blouse.
5. I'm looking for an umbrella.
6. Blouses are over there.

Answers

1. shirt
2. coats
3. suits
4. blouse
5. umbrella
6. blouses

C. WHAT ARE THEY SAYING?

1. coat, Coats
2. jacket, Jackets
3. belt, Belts
4. sweater, Sweaters
5. suit, Suits
6. blouse, Blouses
7. umbrella, Umbrellas
8. necklace, Necklaces

A. WHAT'S THE WORD?

1. shoes
2. jeans
3. gloves
4. socks
5. pajamas
6. mittens

B. LISTENING

Listen and put a check under the correct picture.

1. I'm looking for a black suit.
2. I'm looking for jeans and a sweater.
3. I'm looking for a pair of pajamas.
4. I'm looking for a pair of gloves.

Answers

1. __ ✓
2. __ ✓
3. ✓ __
4. __ ✓

C. MATCHING

1. c
2. d
3. a
4. b
5. f
6. e
7. k
8. j
9. i
10. l
11. h
12. g

D. WORD SEARCH

(See page 155.)

E. WHICH ONE DOESN'T BELONG?

1. shirt (The others are worn below the waist.)
2. socks (The others are worn on the hands.)
3. tie (The others are only for women.)
4. skirt (The others are jewelry items.)
5. socks (The others are worn above the waist.)
6. coat (The others are worn on the feet.)

A. MISSING LETTERS

1. green
2. red
3. yellow
4. orange
5. purple
6. blue
7. black
8. white
9. pink
10. brown
11. gray

B. WHAT'S THE COLOR?

1. red
2. green
3. yellow
4. orange
5. white
6. brown

C. LISTENING

Listen and circle the word you hear.

1. A. What's your favorite color?
   B. My favorite color is yellow.
2. A. What's your favorite color?
   B. My favorite color is green.
3. A. What's your favorite color?
   B. My favorite color is pink.
4. A. What's your favorite color?
   B. My favorite color is brown.
5. A. What's your favorite color?
   B. My favorite color is red.
6. A. What's your favorite color?
   B. My favorite color is purple.

Answers

1. yellow
2. green
3. pink
4. brown
5. red
6. purple

A. WHICH GROUP?

Clothing	Size	Color
coat	extra-large	blue
dress	large	brown
gloves	medium	green
jacket	size 34	orange
mittens	small	red
pants	size 10	yellow

B. LISTENING

Listen and circle the word you hear.

1. A. I'm looking for a sweater.
   B. What size?
   A. Large.

2. A. May I help you?
   B. Yes. I'm looking for a brown jacket.

3. A. I'm looking for a dress.
   B. What size?
   A. Size 11.

4. A. What's the matter with the coat?
   B. It's too long.

5. A. May I help you?
   B. Yes. I'm looking for a pair of shoes.
   A. What size?
   B. Size 5.

6. A. What's the matter with the blouse?
   B. It's too small.

Answers

1.	large	4.	long
2.	brown	5.	5
3.	11	6.	small

C. MATCHING

1. over there.
2. black jacket.
3. is too big.
4. 12.
5. are too tight.
6. gray socks.

WORKBOOK PAGE 81

A. WHAT'S THE PRICE?

1. Shirts
2. Ties
3. Belts
4. Pants
5. Necklaces
6. Dresses
7. Gloves
8. Watches
9. Shoes
10. Umbrellas

B. MATCHING PRICES

1.	$10.15	4.	$25.45
2.	$10.50	5.	$25.54
3.	$50.10		

C. LISTENING

Listen and circle the price you hear.

1. A. What's the price of the shoes?
   B. Forty-five dollars.

2. A. What's the price of the pants?
   B. Thirty-six dollars.

3. A. What's the price of the watches?
   B. Sixty-one dollars.

4. A. What's the price of the ties?
   B. Nineteen fifty.

5. A. What's the price of the sweaters?
   B. Sixty dollars.

6. A. What's the price of the belts?
   B. Nineteen ninety-nine.

7. A. What's the price of the jeans?
   B. Eighteen dollars and seventy-seven cents.

8. A. What's the price of the suits?
   B. Ninety-six fifty.

9. A. What's the price of the skirts?
   B. Thirty two sixty-five.

Answers

1.	$45.00	6.	$19.99
2.	$36.00	7.	$18.77
3.	$61.00	8.	$96.50
4.	$19.50	9.	$32.65
5.	$60.00		

WORKBOOK PAGE 82

A. MATCHING

1. He's old.
2. He's short.
3. He's divorced.
4. Large.
5. Twenty-five dollars.

B. WHICH WORD?

1.	Vietnam	6.	can
2.	height	7.	socks
3.	blue	8.	eggs
4.	Arabic	9.	small
5.	banana	10.	bread

C. LISTENING

Listen and circle the words you hear.

1. A. Are you hungry?
   B. Yes. I'm very hungry.

2. A. Where are the blouses?
   B. Blouses are over there.

3. A. What's he wearing?
   B. He's wearing a blue suit.

4. A. What language do you speak?
   B. I speak Korean.

5. A. What's the matter with the pants?
   B. They're too long.

Answers

1.	hungry	4.	Korean
2.	blouses	5.	long
3.	blue suit		

WORKBOOK PAGES 83–84

A. MATCHING

1.	g	5.	b
2.	e	6.	c
3.	f	7.	a
4.	d		

B. LISTENING

Listen and write the number next to the correct picture.

1. A. Where's the deposit slip?
   B. Here it is.

2. A. Where's the withdrawal slip?
   B. Here it is.

3. A. Where's the bank book?
   B. Here it is.

4. A. Where's the checkbook?
   B. Here it is.

5. A. Where's the credit card?
   B. Here it is.

6. A. Where's the ATM card?
   B. Here it is.

Answers

3	1	4
6	2	5

C. CROSSWORD

(See page 155.)

A. MATCHING

1. forty-seven twenty-five.
2. seventy-five dollars.
3. sixty-five ninety.
4. one hundred fifty dollars.
5. sixteen dollars and ten cents.
6. ninety-five fifteen.

B. WRITE THE CHECKS

1. Two hundred fifty dollars and 00/100
2. Seventy dollars and 0/100
3. Forty-five dollars and 15/100
4. Four hundred seventy-one dollars and 30/100
5. Eighty-three dollars and 99/100

A. MATCHING

1. package
2. money order
3. stamps
4. registered letter
5. air letter

B. WHICH WORD?

1. stamps
2. an air letter
3. a package
4. a registered letter
5. mail

C. LISTENING

Listen and circle the word you hear.

1. I want to mail a package.
2. Where can I buy stamps?
3. Excuse me. Where can I buy a money order?
4. I want to mail this letter.
5. When does the post office open?
6. You can send registered letters at window number 7.

Answers

1. package
2. stamps
3. money order
4. letter

5. open
6. 7

D. AN ENVELOPE

1. Elizabeth Chen
2. 1200 Lake Avenue
   Miami, FL 74354

A. HOW MUCH MONEY?

1. $50.00, $4.50
2. $20.00, $4.00
3. $70.00, $6.50
4. $40.00, $7.45
5. $30.00, $3.20
6. $80.00, $8.75
7. $15.00, $1.90
8. $100.00, $5.60
9. $13.00, $.05

B. LISTENING

Listen and circle the correct amount.

1. A. That's ten dollars and fifty cents.
   B. Here's twenty.
   A. Your change is nine dollars and fifty cents.

2. A. That's six dollars and eighty-six cents.
   B. Here's ten.
   A. Your change is three dollars and fourteen cents.

3. A. That's seventy-three ten.
   B. Here's eighty.
   A. Your change is six dollars and ninety cents.

4. A. That's thirty-nine dollars and seventy cents.
   B. Here's forty.
   A. Your change is thirty cents.

5. A. That's eighty-two eighty-five.
   B. Here's ninety.
   A. Your change is seven dollars and fifteen cents.

6. A. That's thirty-eight dollars and twenty cents.
   B. Here's fifty.
   A. Your change is eleven dollars and eighty cents.

Answers

1. $9.50   4. $.30
2. $3.14   5. $7.15
3. $6.90   6. $11.80

A. WHAT'S THE WORD?

1. headache
2. backache
3. stomachache
4. cold
5. earache
6. toothache
7. sore throat
8. cough
9. fever

B. LISTENING

Listen and write the number under the correct picture.

1. I have a backache.
2. I have a sore throat.
3. I have a cold.
4. I have a headache.
5. I have a stomachache.

Answers

5   3   2   1   4

C. WHICH WORD?

1. have   5. have
2. has   6. has
3. have   7. has, have
4. has

D. LISTENING

Listen and circle the word you hear.

1. A. What's the matter?
   B. My neck hurts.

2. A. What's the matter?
   B. My foot hurts.

3. A. What's the matter?
   B. My leg hurts.

4. A. What's the matter?
   B. My ear hurts.

5. A. What's the matter?
   B. My hand hurts.

6. A. What's the matter?
   B. My eye hurts.

Answers

1. neck
2. foot
3. leg
4. ear
5. hand
6. eye

E. WORD SEARCH

(See page 155.)

WORKBOOK PAGES 92–94

A. MATCHING

1. You should use aspirin.
2. You should use antacid tablets.
3. You should use cold medicine.
4. You should use throat lozenges.
5. You should use cough syrup.
6. You should use ear drops.

B. LISTENING

Listen and write the number under the correct picture.

1. I have a cough. What should I use?
2. I have a cold. What should I use?
3. I have a stomachache. What should I use?
4. I have a headache. What should I use?
5. I have an earache. What should I use?
6. I have a sore throat. What should I use?

Answers

3   1   4   6   2   5

C. CROSSWORD

(See page 156.)

D. WHICH ONE DOESN'T BELONG?

1. throat lozenges (The others are ailments.)
2. cold (The others are medicines.)
3. cough syrup (The others are ailments.)
4. fever (The others are "aches.")
5. medicine (The others are ailments.)

E. WHERE CAN I FIND THEM?

1. cold medicine
2. antacid tablets

3. cough syrup
4. ear drops
5. aspirin
6. throat lozenges

F. MATCHING

1. medicine
2. lozenges
3. tablets
4. syrup

G. LISTENING

Listen and circle the words you hear.

1. Excuse me. Where can I find antacid tablets?
2. Excuse me. Where can I find cough syrup?
3. Look in Aisle 5.
4. I have an earache.
5. Cold medicine is in Aisle 7.
6. Excuse me. Where can I find throat lozenges?

Answers

1. antacid tablets
2. cough syrup
3. Aisle 5
4. earache
5. Aisle 7
6. throat lozenges

WORKBOOK PAGES 95–96

A. WHAT'S THE WORD?

1. Doctor's
2. Hello
3. appointment
4. problem
5. headache
6. today
7. 2:00

B. WHAT'S THE ANSWER?

1. You should use ear drops.
2. My back hurts.
3. Look in Aisle 11.
4. Yes, that's fine.

C. MATCHING

1. I cut my face.
2. I broke my arm.
3. I burned my hand.
4. I broke my leg.
5. I sprained my wrist.
6. I cut my finger.

D. LISTENING

Listen and circle the word you hear.

1. I broke my arm.
2. I cut my face.
3. I sprained my wrist.
4. I burned my hand.
5. I cut my arm.
6. I'm sorry to hear that.

Answers

1. arm
2. face
3. sprained
4. burned
5. arm
6. hear

WORKBOOK PAGE 97

A. MATCHING

1. thirty minutes every day.
2. three healthy meals a day.
3. six glasses of water a day.
4. one vitamin every day.
5. eight hours every day.

B. HOW ABOUT YOU?

1. exercise
2. drink
3. sleep
4. take
5. eat

C. WHAT'S THE WORD?

1. Operator
2. hurt
3. head
4. ambulance
5. address
6. number

WORKBOOK PAGES 98–99

A. CROSSWORD

(See page 156.)

B. LISTENING

Listen and choose the correct answer.

1. Take two tablets once a day.
2. Take three pills twice a day.
3. Take two caplets three times a day.
4. Take two teaspoons before meals.
5. Take one caplet after meals.
6. Take four caplets twice a day.

Answers

1. b
2. a
3. b
4. a
5. b
6. b

147

C. WHAT'S THE DOSAGE?

1. one, once
2. two, twice
3. two, once
4. caplets, meal

WORKBOOK PAGES 100–101

A. WHO ARE THEY?

1. principal
2. English teacher
3. P.E. teacher
4. guidance counselor
5. school nurse
6. custodian

B. WHAT'S THE WORD?

1. office
2. cafeteria
3. gym
4. nurse's office
5. library

C. LISTENING

Listen and circle the words you hear.

1. Excuse me. Where's the guidance office?
2. The students are in the auditorium.
3. Hello. I'm the new school librarian.
4. I'm going to the nurse's office.
5. I'm looking for the custodian.
6. I'm the new P.E. teacher.

Answers

1. guidance office
2. auditorium
3. librarian
4. nurse's office
5. custodian
6. P.E. teacher

D. WHICH ONE DOESN'T BELONG?

1. principal (The others are places.)
2. principal's office (The others are people.)
3. gym (The others are "offices.")
4. library (The others are people.)

E. CROSSWORD

(See page 156.)

WORKBOOK PAGE 102

A. WHAT'S THE WORD?

1. English
2. science
3. art
4. technology
5. social studies
6. music
7. math

B. LISTENING

Listen and circle the word you hear.

1. My favorite subject is music.
2. My favorite subject is social studies.
3. My favorite subject is science.
4. My favorite subject is math.
5. My favorite subject is art.
6. My favorite subject is technology.

Answers

1. music
2. social studies
3. science
4. math
5. art
6. technology

WORKBOOK PAGE 103

A. WHAT'S THE WORD?

1. choir
2. orchestra
3. basketball
4. band
5. football
6. drama

B. WHICH GROUP?

People at School
guidance counselor
librarian
school nurse

Places at School
auditorium
gym
library

School Subjects
English
social studies
technology

Extracurricular Activities
band
drama
orchestra

WORKBOOK PAGE 104

A. MATCHING

1. second period, Room 211
2. third period, Ms. Chang
3. fourth period, science
4. first period, Room 134
5. sixth period, art
6. fifth period, music

B. MY CLASS SCHEDULE

1. fourth, one twenty-eight
2. fifth, fourteen
3. sixth, two seventeen
4. second, two eleven
5. first, one thirty-four
6. third, three forty-one

C. LISTENING

Listen and circle the number you hear.

1. I have social studies second period.
2. I have English third period.
3. I have technology fifth period.
4. I have science first period.
5. My music class is in Room 314.
6. My art class is in Room 509.

Answers

1. second	4. first
2. third	5. 314
3. fifth	6. 509

WORKBOOK PAGE 105

A. MATCHING

1. 3 times a day.
2. 9:30.
3. 8 hours every day.
4. Room 219.
5. Aisle 3.

B. WHICH WORD?

1. deposit
2. check
3. mail

4. throat
5. antacid tablets
6. custodian
7. social studies
8. finger
9. exercise

C. LISTENING

Listen and circle the word you hear.

1. A. Your change is seven dollars and thirty cents.
   B. Thank you.

2. A. What's the matter?
   B. My neck hurts.

3. A. What happened?
   B. I burned my hand.

4. A. Who's that?
   B. That's the librarian.

5. A. What's your favorite subject?
   B. My favorite subject is science.

6. A. What are you going to do after school today?
   B. I have drama practice.

Answers

1. $7.30
2. neck
3. burned
4. librarian
5. science
6. drama

WORKBOOK PAGES 106–107

A. WHAT'S THE OCCUPATION?

1. delivery person
2. custodian
3. cashier
4. police officer
5. electrician
6. cook
7. construction worker
8. security guard
9. repairperson
10. gardener

B. LISTENING

Listen and put a check under the correct picture.

1. A. What do you do?
   B. I'm a delivery person.

2. A. What do you do?
   B. I'm a cook.

3. A. What do you do?
   B. I'm a police officer.

4. A. What do you do?
   B. I'm an electrician.

5. A. What do you do?
   B. I'm a custodian.

6. A. What do you do?
   B. I'm a security guard.

Answers

1. ___ ✓
2. ✓ ___
3. ✓ ___
4. ___ ✓
5. ___ ✓
6. ✓ ___

C. MATCHING

1. person
2. worker
3. guard
4. officer

WORKBOOK PAGE 108

A. MATCHING

1. repairs buildings.
2. paints.
3. fixes cars.
4. drives a truck.
5. types.
6. bakes.
7. drives a bus.
8. teaches.
9. fixes sinks.
10. drives a taxi.

B. LISTENING

Listen and write the number under the correct picture.

1. I can drive a bus.
2. I can teach.
3. I can repair buildings.
4. I'm an experienced truck driver.
5. I'm an experienced painter.
6. I'm an experienced baker.
7. I can type.
8. I'm an experienced plumber.

Answers

| 5 | 1 | 3 | 7 |
| 8 | 6 | 2 | 4 |

WORKBOOK PAGES 109–110

A. WHERE DO THEY WORK?

1. a salesperson, Dan's Department Store
2. a pharmacist, ABC Pharmacy
3. a waiter, the Harbor Restaurant
4. a doctor, Bayside Hospital
5. an assembler, O.K. Electronics
6. a housekeeper, the Carlson Hotel

B. LISTENING

Listen and circle the correct occupation.

1. I work at the Royal Hotel.
2. I work at Marcy's Department Store.
3. I work at Randy's Restaurant.
4. I work at Ajax Electronics.
5. I work at the Westville Hospital.
6. I work at Central Pharmacy.

Answers

1. housekeeper
2. salesperson
3. waiter
4. assembler
5. doctor
6. pharmacist

C. CROSSWORD

(See page 156.)

D. WHICH ONE DOESN'T BELONG?

1. pharmacist (The others are places.)
2. restaurant (The others are people.)
3. housekeeper (The others are "drivers.")
4. custodian (The others are places.)
5. restaurant (The others are people.)

WORKBOOK PAGE 111

A. WHICH WORD?

1. assemble
2. cut
3. operate
4. repair
5. use
6. sell

B. LISTENING

Listen and put a check under the correct picture.

1. A. Can you use a cash register?
   B. No, I can't. But I'm sure I can learn quickly.

2. A. Can you assemble components?
   B. No, I can't. But I'm sure I can learn quickly.

3. A. Can you cut hair?
   B. No, I can't. But I'm sure I can learn quickly.

4. A. Can you sell watches?
   B. No, I can't. But I'm sure I can learn quickly.

Answers

1. ✓ __
2. ✓ __
3. __ ✓
4. __ ✓

WORKBOOK PAGES 112–113

A. MATCHING

1. The personnel office is down the hall.
2. The cafeteria is down the hall.
3. The supply room is down the hall.
4. The employee lounge is down the hall.
5. The bathroom is down the hall.
6. The vending machine is down the hall.
7. The mailroom is down the hall.

B. LISTENING

Listen and circle the word you hear.

1. Excuse me. Where's the mailroom?
2. I'm looking for the cafeteria.
3. The employee lounge is down the hall.
4. Excuse me. Where's the supply room?
5. The vending machine is down the hall.

Answers

1. mailroom
2. cafeteria
3. employee lounge
4. supply room
5. down

C. WORD SEARCH

(See page 156.)

D. WHAT'S THE LOCATION?

(See page 156.)

WORKBOOK PAGE 114

A. WHAT'S THE WORD?

1. wet
2. safety
3. smoke
4. room
5. Thanks
6. Careful

B. WHICH GROUP?

Occupations
custodian
gardener
security guard

Locations at Work
mailroom
personnel office
supply room

Work Skills
drive a bus
paint
repair buildings

Work Sites
Buy-Rite Pharmacy
Grover Hospital
Hi-Tech Electronics

WORKBOOK PAGE 115

A. KENJI'S WORK SCHEDULE

1. six
2. Thursday
3. four
4. five
5. seven
6. Friday
7. thirty-five

B. PAYCHECK DEDUCTIONS

1. $520.00
2. $26.00
3. $52.00
4. $24.50
5. $41.60
6. $144.10
7. $375.90

C. LISTENING

Listen and circle the numbers you hear.

1. I work every day from 9 AM to 5 PM.
2. I make fifteen dollars an hour.
3. I work forty hours a week.
4. Every month I pay twenty-seven fifty for my company's health plan.
5. My gross pay is six hundred dollars.
6. After deductions, I take home four hundred and fifteen dollars a month.

Answers

1. 9 AM to 5 PM
2. $15.00
3. 40 hours
4. $27.50
5. $600.00
6. $415.00

WORKBOOK PAGES 116–117

A. WHAT'S THE LOCATION?

1. right, next to
2. left, across from
3. left, next to
4. right, across from

B. LISTENING

Listen and write the names on the buildings.

1. The post office is on the right, across from the bank.
2. The bakery is on the left, next to the bank.
3. The library is on the right, next to the clinic.
4. The movie theater is on the right, next to the library.
5. The drug store is on the left, across from the movie theater.
6. The train station is on the left, next to the drug store.
7. The laundromat is on the right, across from the train station.

Answers

(See page 156.)

C. YES OR NO?

1. Yes
2. No
3. Yes
4. Yes
5. No
6. No
7. Yes

A. WHERE DO THEY GO?

1. Take Bus Number 12.
2. Take the B Train.
3. Take Bus Number 2.
4. Take the C Train.
5. Take Bus Number 11.
6. Take the Blue Line.

B. LISTENING

Listen and circle the correct answer.

1. A. Excuse me. How do I get to Franklin Square?
   B. Take the D Train.
   A. The D Train?
   B. Yes. That's right.

2. A. Excuse me. How do I get to City Hall?
   B. Take Bus Number 5.
   A. Bus Number 5?
   B. Yes. That's right.

3. A. Excuse me. How do I get to Jefferson Street?
   B. Take the Yellow Line.
   A. The Yellow Line?
   B. Yes. That's right.

4. A. Excuse me. How do I get to the airport?
   B. Take Bus M7.
   A. Bus M7?
   B. Yes. That's right.

5. A. Excuse me. How do I get to Central Avenue?
   B. Take the Green Line.
   A. The C Line?
   B. No. The Green Line.
   A. Oh. Thank you.

6. A. Excuse me. How do I get to the zoo?
   B. The zoo?
   A. Yes.
   B. Take Bus Number 22.
   A. Thank you.

Answers

1. the D Train
2. Bus Number 5
3. the Yellow Line
4. Bus M7
5. the Green Line
6. Bus Number 22

A. MATCHING

1. Get off at Eleventh Avenue.
2. Get off at Center Street.
3. Get off at Central Avenue.
4. Get off at Sixth Street.
5. Get off at Fifth Street.
6. Get off at Seventh Avenue.

B. LISTENING

Listen and put a check under the correct street sign.

1. A. Excuse me. Where do I get off for the library?
   B. Get off at First Avenue.
   A. Thanks very much.

2. A. Excuse me. Where do I get off for the Plaza Mall?
   B. Get off at Pine Street.
   A. Thanks very much.

3. A. Excuse me. Where do I get off for the zoo?
   B. Get off at Second Street.
   A. Thanks very much.

4. A. Excuse me. Where do I get off for the Westville Clinic?
   D. Get off at Day Street.
   A. Thanks very much.

5. A. Excuse me. Where do I get off for the post office?
   B. Get off at C Street.
   A. Thanks very much.

6. A. Excuse me. Where do I get off for the airport?
   B. Get off at West Avenue.
   A. Thanks very much.

Answers

1. ✓ __
2. ✓ __
3. __ ✓
4. __ ✓
5. ✓ __
6. __ ✓

A. MATCHING

1. Slow down! The sign says, "Speed Limit 30."
2. You have to stop!
3. You can't go that way!
4. You can't go on that street!
5. Don't turn yet!

B. LISTENING

Listen and put a check under the correct sign.

1. Slow down! The sign says, "Speed Limit 35."
2. You have to stop!
3. You can't go on that street!
4. You can't go that way!
5. You're driving too fast!
6. Don't turn yet!

Answers

1. __ ✓
2. ✓ __
3. __ ✓
4. __ ✓
5. ✓ __
6. __ ✓

C. WHAT'S THE WORD?

1. U
2. right
3. left
4. train
5. people
6. school

D. LISTENING

Listen and circle the words you hear.

1. The sign says, "No right turn."
2. The sign says, "No U-turn."
3. Slow down! There are people in the street.
4. Slow down! There's a school nearby.
5. Slow down! There are train tracks ahead!

Answers

1. right
2. U-turn
3. people
4. school
5. train tracks

A. BUS NUMBER 6B

1. Day Street, Sixth Avenue
2. 5:45
3. 6:00
4. 6:45, 7:15
5. 8:45, 9:30
6. 10:45
7. 9:15, 9:45

B. LISTENING

Listen to sentences about the schedule above. Circle the correct answers.

1. The first bus in the morning arrives at Main Street at six o'clock.
2. It arrives at Sixth Avenue at six thirty.
3. The second bus in the morning leaves Day Street at six forty-five.
4. It arrives at Pine Street at seven thirty.
5. The last bus leaves Day Street at nine o'clock.
6. It arrives at Fifth Avenue at nine thirty.
7. It's ten fifteen. The next bus leaves Day Street at ten forty-five.
8. It arrives at Sixth Avenue at eleven thirty.
9. It's two thirty. The next bus leaves Day Street at three forty-five.
10. It arrives at Main Street at four fifteen.

Answers

1. Yes	6. Yes
2. No	7. Yes
3. Yes	8. No
4. No	9. Yes
5. No	10. No

A. WHAT'S THE ACTIVITY?

1. go swimming
2. go jogging
3. exercise
4. play tennis
5. go dancing
6. play basketball
7. watch TV
8. go rollerblading
9. listen to music
10. play soccer

B. CROSSWORD

(See page 156.)

C. LISTENING

Listen and write the number under the correct picture.

1. I like to play basketball.
2. I like to go swimming.
3. I like to watch TV.
4. I like to play tennis.
5. I like to listen to music.
6. I like to go dancing.
7. I like to play soccer.
8. I like to exercise.

Answers

4	8	2	1
3	5	7	6

A. MATCHING

1. c	6. f
2. b	7. h
3. g	8. e
4. a	9. i
5. d	

B. LISTENING

Listen and put a check under the correct picture.

1. A. What are you going to do tomorrow?
   B. I'm going to go jogging.
2. A. What are you going to do tomorrow?
   B. I'm going to go to the zoo.
3. A. What are you going to do tomorrow?
   B. I'm going to see a play.
4. A. What are you going to do tomorrow?
   B. I'm going to go to a ballgame.
5. A. What are you going to do tomorrow?
   B. I'm going to see a movie.
6. A. What are you going to do tomorrow?
   B. I'm going to play soccer.

Answers

1. ✓ ___
2. ___ ✓
3. ___ ✓
4. ✓ ___
5. ___ ✓
6. ✓ ___

C. WHAT'S THE WORD?

1. go	4. see
2. see	5. go
3. play	6. play

A. WHAT DID YOU DO YESTERDAY?

1. listened	4. exercised
2. watched	5. went
3. played	6. saw

B. LISTENING

Listen and put a check under the correct picture.

1. A. What did you do yesterday?
   B. I watched TV.
2. A. What did you do yesterday?
   B. I went swimming.
3. A. What did you do yesterday?
   B. I played soccer.
4. A. What did you do yesterday?
   B. I listened to music.
5. A. What did you do yesterday?
   B. I saw a play.
6. A. What did you do yesterday?
   B. I went to a ballgame.

Answers

1. ✓ ___
2. ✓ ___
3. ___ ✓
4. ✓ ___
5. ___ ✓
6. ✓ ___

C. MATCHING

1. tennis.
2. a concert.
3. TV.

4. a movie.
5. the park.
6. baseball.
7. music.
8. soccer.
9. swimming.
10. rollerblading.
11. golf.
12. a play.

D. WHICH ONE DOESN'T BELONG?

1. exercised (The others are sports people "played.")
2. listened to music (The others are places people "went.")
3. watched TV (The others are outside the home.)
4. went to the park (The others are indoor activities.)
5. went jogging (The others are activities where people sat.)

WORKBOOK PAGE 130

A. MATCHING

1. five days a week.
2. three times a week.
3. twice a week.
4. once a week.
5. twice a month.
6. on the 2nd Saturday in June.
7. on the 4th Saturday in June.

B. LISTENING

Listen and circle the words you hear.

1. I work five days a week.
2. I go swimming twice a month.
3. I play golf three times a week.
4. I'm going to go to a play on May seventh.
5. I'm going to go to a concert on August fourth.
6. I'm going to go dancing on the first Friday in December.

Answers

1. five days
2. twice
3. three times
4. May 7th
5. August 4th
6. 1st Friday

WORKBOOK PAGE 131

A. MATCHING

1. I'm an electrician.
2. I can paint.
3. I saw a play.
4. Down the hall.
5. Take the Blue Line.

B. WHICH WORD?

1. gardener
2. truck driver
3. can't
4. safety glasses
5. tomorrow

6. yesterday
7. week
8. go
9. right

C. LISTENING

Listen and circle the words you hear.

1. A. Can you bake?
   B. Yes. I'm a very experienced baker.
2. A. I can't come to work today. I'm sick.
   B. I hope you feel better soon.
3. A. How do I get to the mall?
   B. Take Bus Number Seventeen.
4. A. What do you like to do in your free time?
   B. I like to go dancing.
5. A. What did you do yesterday?
   B. I played soccer.
6. A. Do you like to play tennis?
   B. Yes. I play tennis twice a week.

Answers

1. baker
2. can't
3. Bus Number 17
4. go dancing
5. played
6. twice

WORKBOOK PAGE 4

WORKBOOK PAGE 5

WORKBOOK PAGE 6

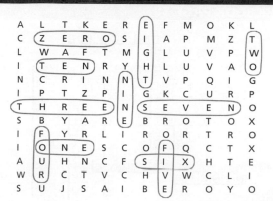

WORKBOOK PAGE 8

NAME	Bernardo [1]			Ortiz	[2]
	First			Last	
ADDRESS	5 [3]	Rowley Street			4C [4]
	Number	Street			Apartment Number
	Easterly [5]		NM [6]	10375 [7]	
	City		State	Zip Code	
TELEPHONE	629 [8]	791-2864 [9]			
	Area Code	Number			

WORKBOOK PAGE 17

```
A L T K E R M E F M O K F
C E L E V E N I T P M Z E
T H R T E F N E W E L E L
I F E T H I R T E E N L E
N I R T H F R T L E N N V
E F I F T T L E V U C U E
I T R I E E S E V E N E N
G S I X T E E N R O T T T
H F Y T L N B R O R T W O
T S E V E N T E E N C E X
E U H E C F A S I X H N E
E R N I N E T E E N C T I
N U J N I N T E E N O Y O
```

WORKBOOK PAGE 20

```
    B     T V
    R     E
  D R E S S E D
    A     T
  W O R K   H O M E A T
    K     A     T
    F     I
    A S H O W E R
    S
    T
```

WORKBOOK PAGE 26

```
T S U N P T M U R S S O
O B C O L D N O A U H R
F C L L S N O W I N G N
O K P T O O T H I N N E
G S E C L O U D I N T H
G N A Y E R A A N Y T N
Y O R U H E F C G V E T
O U A S O A O H A O K S
U W C I S T C L O U D Y
```

WORKBOOK PAGE 30

```
      T H I R T E E N
      H
    F O R T Y - S I X       O
      R     I           N
    T W E N T Y     F   E
      G     T     F I F T E E N   H
      H     Y - S I X T E E N     U
    N I N E T Y   T W E L V E     N
            E     V           D
            N     E           R
                 F           E
                 O           D
                 U
                 R
```

WORKBOOK PAGE 32

```
S U N D A Y I M E F T O K L A
T H U R D A Y M S O U E D A Y W
M O N D U Y M U E S D A Y T Y
L O T O N R Y N A V I D A Y Y M
W E N S D T N D A Y W S G M O D
C D P D S H U I Y E E A S O D A
H A Z O T U N Y D E D T E Y
B Y B H R E R T R O N O T U R
W E D N E S D A Y O R E R U R D A Y
S A T O R D A Y E F S D R D A Y
F A T U S A F A D I R D A L
F R I A D Y H U A S I A Y A N
P S U D A Y I O F R I D A Y L N
T U E D Y Y N A Y P A E C B N
W E D N D A Y G R I Y Z M A H
```

WORKBOOK PAGE 35

```
  S E V E N T E E N T H
  I     W
  X     E L E V E N T H
  T     N     H
  I   F I F T I E T H I
  E   O   I   R
  T   U   E   D
  H   R   T
      T   H
      E
    N I N E T I E T H
      N
    T W E L F T H
      H
```

WORKBOOK PAGE 36

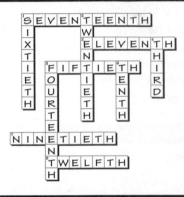

WORKBOOK PAGE 43

```
D E S H L K S C L O S E T P
K I T C H E N A G L U V P W
L I O E N R Y A H L U V A B W
E N V E I F I R E P L A C E B
C I E T Z P I L G K C U R D E
H S Z O P A N E R E B E W D
C H B Y B A T H R O O M O R
W O S H O W R B R O R T R O
A W O N A S C N O F C C T O
F E U H B C F A S I L H T M
Q R C D V B E F E R M M P E
P S U J O W I F E E S T Y I
S W I N D O W N A Y P E E C B
T E R O B C K G R I T Z M A
```

WORKBOOK PAGE 48

```
I B R B R I M E F M O K
H G L I B R A R Y S P O R
G W R T T M B A N S S D J O
R O T E A R Y A N S A T R E
O C L T C L N I C D R E D L
C Z O O A N E Y E V D N A
E B A Y N G R O C R Y N M U
R K U N D O R M A T E S A N
Y A S T A T I O F S S R Y D
S E S A R T S T A R Y R
T Y T N H B A K R Y O
O R R C E R Y E E Y M
R B A N K A Y P R E A
E B U S S T A T I O N
```

WORKBOOK PAGE 54

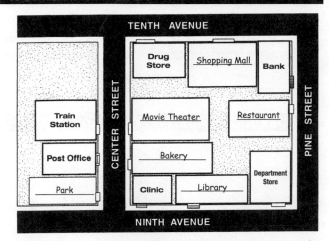

WORKBOOK PAGE 60

```
L I B R D R I S I K M O K
D H G R E W E N T M J U R
S A F R A I D U A N S D A K S
R H U N G B W R N C E E I
T U C L R T I B E D P Y G C
H N P T N I B E A N G R Y K
U G Z O G F Y A P D V D Y C
N R B Y S A D Y P O R T U
R Y A U Y E R M Y U T I R P
Y S T H A G R I O F B E D S
F B S M A R R I E D S I E
Q D A Y E N H U A S K T O
S I N G L E R R Y E H K R
A L I N R Y N T H I R S T Y
D I R O D H M A R T Y O R E
```

WORKBOOK PAGE 69

```
H L R P M N R Y S T P R J
J C A N T M U A N S O A A
I A N Q R Y L O A F U E G
R L O F F I S R A R N G N
N P T A I B U B O D B U E
P O U N D R B O T U R Y H
O O T L L R S B U N C H Y
U W U B E R Q A R Y H S E
D M B O T T L E F B L O D
N D I T S T Y S T L B A O
J A R T N H B A X K A G Z
S T I E E D R B O T L R E
L I N L Q U A R T R G N
C A M E D O Z N E Y O R E
```

WORKBOOK PAGE 71

WORKBOOK PAGE 78

```
I B B N A D S E F M O K C
H B L O U S E P C O A R A
H W N P T M J A N S D J O
J E E N S C K T S C O A T
I S S C R P K B N O O S J J
J H O M N R E Y P A N T S
I I L S S T S H A O E R S
C R T I K T R O M J E S I
D S S I I T S M A M Y K U
T D E R R L S S A R I T
S H O E S J U I T E A A
S G R T J N I S S E Y T
W A T C H N T S O W K D P
```

WORKBOOK PAGE 84

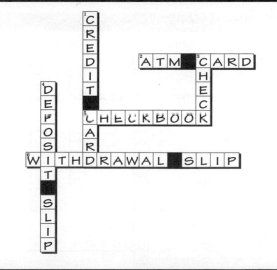

WORKBOOK PAGE 91

```
L A C H H E A D T H R O T E
S H L T O O T R Y S T P R H
T C O L D T A H E D A C H E
O E A N Q S R F E V E R S
C A U G H L I S R A R N G T
A C P S T E M A H C R E R O
T O O T H A C H E T T E Y M
Y U H Y E R A A O T H A A A
C G E U B A C A C H E T Y C
O H A S O C H H A C K S S H
U T D I T H T Y S I L O A A
G D A Y H E A D A C H E C
S O R E T H R O A T D H R H
C L I N E Y N A Y P R E E E
Z E R A C H B A C K A C H E
```

WORKBOOK PAGE 93

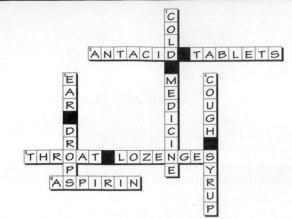

Crossword answers:
1. COLD MEDICINE
2. ANTACID TABLETS
3. EAR DROPS
4. COUGH SYRUP
5. THROAT LOZENGES
6. ASPIRIN

WORKBOOK PAGE 98

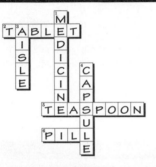

Crossword answers:
1. TABLET
2. AISLE
3. MEDICINE
4. CAPSULE
5. TEASPOON
6. PILL

WORKBOOK PAGE 101

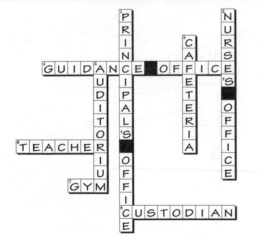

Crossword answers:
1. PRINCIPAL'S OFFICE
2. NURSE'S OFFICE
3. CAFETERIA
4. GUIDANCE OFFICE
5. AUDITORIUM
6. TEACHER
7. GYM
8. CUSTODIAN

WORKBOOK PAGE 110

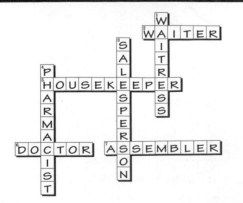

Crossword answers:
1. WAITER
2. WAITRESS
3. SALESPERSON
4. PHARMACIST
5. HOUSEKEEPER
6. DOCTOR
7. ASSEMBLER

WORKBOOK PAGE 113

```
L A C H B A T R O O H C S F
S U P L Y R O O M T I T P N B
E M S B E R C R A I B P N B D
C A F E T E R I A T H M P B D
E I C L O N A K L B O A O Q
E L U K O O T H C I H O R N G
N R O M T R O R M W V D E G J
D O M A L I N G R O O M M
I P C A F O B L B T A R H
I O S K E M P L O Y E E R H
E M P L O Y E E L O U N G E
B G M L R O O B T H R E O E
V E N D I N G M A C H I N E
```

WORKBOOK PAGE 113

mailroom	supply room	employee lounge
bathroom	personnel office	cafeteria

WORKBOOK PAGE 117

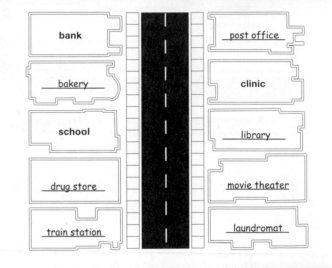

bank
bakery
school
drug store
train station
post office
clinic
library
movie theater
laundromat

WORKBOOK PAGE 124

Crossword answers:
1. PLAY TENNIS
2. GO DANCING
3. GO JOGGING
4. PLAY SOCCER
5. PLAY BASKETBALL
5. GO SWIMMING
6. WATCH TV
7. GO ROLLERBLADING